"Succession planning is the best gift a leader can give to their company—but it's not simple. In this book, Beth digs deep into the intentional phases leaders need to walk through to ensure the continuity of the business you've worked so hard to grow. I highly recommend this regardless of the stage of your business."
—Verne Harnish, Founder Entrepreneurs' Organization (EO) and author of *Scaling Up (Rockefeller Habits 2.0)*

"If you're like most of the leaders I coach, you need this book. Beth nails the pitfalls leaders face when they fail to plan their succession and expertly outlines the phases brilliant leaders can leverage in executing an exit strategy. It's a must read for all business owners!"
—Todd Palmer, 6x INC 5,000 CEO and #1 International Best-Selling Author

"Leaders who build ensuing companies know that leadership is a continuous journey toward irrelevance. Here, Beth Miller shows us how to do that."
—L. David Marquet, Former submarine commander, Author, *Turn the Ship Around!*

"With so much transition happening in the marketplace, this is a timely book for business leaders. No matter what level of leadership you are sitting in, *Replaceable* delivers actionable steps for your succession planning."
—Dee Ann Turner, Author of *Bet on Talent and Crush Your Career*, CEO, Dee Ann Turner & Associates

"Beth Miller has captured the essence of a succession plan and how it should be used in a privately held business. This book focuses on the succession, and she makes sure the reader understands the difference between succession and exiting a business. Read this book and don't fall into the trap of confusing the two."

—Josh Patrick, Author of *Sustainable:*
A Fable About Creating a Personally and Economically
Sustainable Business and *The Sale Ready Company*

"How do you identify top talent and engage them in such a way that you're ensuring a solid succession plan? Beth masterfully breaks this essential process down so any leader can grab hold and run with it. Your team will thank you for reading and applying your learnings from this book."

—Kevin Sheridan, Author of *Building a Magnetic Culture,*
Leading Expert on Employee Engagement, Culture &
Managing Virtual Workers, Keynote Speaker

"Never was a book so needed, and never was the solution so well laid out. When I was a recruiter for closely held companies, I turned down more assignments than I accepted because potential clients had no plan, no roadmap, no process to ensure the executive I was asked to recruit would be successful. Beth has left nothing to chance in this book. She provides a step-by-step, no-fail process for succession and leaving a legacy, just as she has done for her clients. If *Replaceable* had been available, I would have made it required reading for my clients.

—Pat Romboletti, Author, TEDx Speaker,
Career Coach

"If you have the need for a comprehensive succession plan but don't know where to start, now you do! This book gives you a practical roadmap to create a strategic succession plan for you and your business. You will be informed and inspired—and ready to implement your plan."

—Kevin Eikenberry, bestselling author of
Remarkable Leadership and co-founder of
The Remote Leadership Institute

"Smart leaders plan their exit strategy with trusted experts like Beth in their corner. Beth's practical approach to succession planning and execution is a must-have for business leaders in any size organization."

—Laurie Barkman, Business Transition and
M&A Advisor, SmallDotBig, Host of
Succession Stories Podcast

"*Replaceable* is at the top of my list for resources as I educate and assist business owners, helping them plan for and achieve successful exits. If you are looking to awaken the fullest potential in your employees, you'll want to add this to your toolbox."

—Patrick Ungashick, CEO, NAVIX Consultants,
Author of Dancing in the End Zone

"Beth lights your soul on fire in *Replaceable, An Obsession with Succession*. I have researched and tackled succession in addition to self-growth work for years, but Beth's methodology has stuck with me more so than any book I've read. If you're looking to have sustainable, long-term success, this book carves out a practical and an engaging trail for you. It is a book built to last."

—Brad Dalton, Keynote Speaker, Best Selling Author,
Positive Team and Personal Transformation Leader

REPLACEABLE

An Obsession with Succession

BETH ARMKNECHT MILLER

Authorsunite.com

Dedicated to the thousands of business owners who choose the difficult path of launching and building businesses that create the very backbone of our economy. These men and women risk everything and deserve to exit financially secure with employees prepared to grow the company into the future.

ACKNOWLEDGMENTS

Many thanks to the people who have advised and supported me through the process of writing, *Replaceable, An Obsession with Succession.*

To the many business owners and expert speakers within Vistage and the business community who provided me insight into the challenges of succession planning for small businesses, I owe a huge debt of gratitude including: Maura Thomas, Mike Pierce, Evan Cramer, Bruce Peddle, Denny Wilson, Andrew MacKnight, Ken Madden, Kyle Tothill, Marissa Maldonado, Paul Laubach, Kathleen Thompson, Brad Shillito, Chad Baxter, Stella Dowling and David Mathis.

A huge thanks to Eric Holtzclaw and his marketing team at Liger Partners especially Whitney Mendozza and Cynthia Hayes who helped in so many ways from keeping me accountable to my goals and advising me on design, marketing, and promotion. To Ginger Schlanger, thank you, for your listening skills and help coming up with the book title, *Replaceable.*

Finally, I am indebted to the authors and experts who were gracious enough to lend their names to my book project through testimonials including: Verne Harnish, David Marquet, Kevin Eikenberry, Dee Ann Turner, Todd Palmer, Patrick Ungashick, Kevin Sheridan, Josh Patrick, Patricia Romboletti, Brad Dalton, and Laurie Barkman.

CONTENTS

INTRODUCTION TO REPLACEABLE

"A leader's lasting value is measured by succession."
~ John C Maxwell ~

As a business owner, you may have thought about exiting your company in the past, yet there was always something holding you back. Or you might be a leader who wants the opportunity to move into a higher position, but there was no one ready to step in and take your place. If so, then this is the book for you!

I can't count the number of times I have been asked to coach a leader who was not meeting the expectations of their manager. After a brief conversation with the executive sponsor, I found the leader had been promoted into a position before they were assessed for their potential and developed to take on a more important position. As a result, they were ill-prepared to be successful.

These scenarios made me realize how many of my clients and other business owners would benefit from looking at the root cause of their leadership missteps by committing to developing and executing a succession plan. A strategic succession plan identifies successors to key positions in your organization and provides a development road map to prepare them for their next position.

When you follow the process of Strategic Succession Planning, you will be setting your future leaders up for success and ultimately making yourself, the business owner or leader, replaceable.

Replaceable takes you on a journey with Dan, the owner of a professional services company who had a goal to step away from his company in a three-year time period. He followed the six phases of strategic succession planning using the succession planning tools and the four conversations described in *Replaceable*: Talent, Career, Development, and Performance.

Following the six phases brought him to a successful sale of his company with an all-cash deal allowing him to walk away from his business confident the remaining leaders were capable of leading the business into the future.

*A Note to all Leaders

While this book is designed for organizational succession planning, I would be remiss not to point out it can also be helpful to leaders other than the CEO or President. It provides guidance to the leader whose organization does not plan for succession. These leaders understand the importance of building a succession plan for their team or department. Who are these leaders? They are the ones who know developing future leaders will…

- provide them with back up when they are on vacation or sabbatical

- increase retention of their high potentials
- free them up to take on more value-added responsibilities

If you're a leader who wants to build a leadership pipeline, you don't have to wait for your executive team to start the process. You have the power to create a succession planning best practice within your own department. To develop a succession plan that creates successor(s) for your position, you will need the following: a performance management system, an understanding of leadership potential in your department, core competencies, and a development planning system.

This book is not about exit planning. As you will learn, succession planning is a component of exit planning. *Replaceable* also does not address the unique aspects a family business has with succession planning.

What this book does provide is a road map and the necessary tools to create and implement a succession plan so you, the leader, will become *Replaceable*.

CHAPTER 1
A TALE OF TWO COMPANIES

As of late 2020, baby boomers own over two million businesses employing more than twenty-five million people in the United States. Many will be retiring or selling their businesses in the next few years, and for some of these business owners the transaction will be a success. These owners will receive the value from their company to provide them with a secure future and their employees will be secure in their roles. Other owners will be left with little or nothing for their years of hard work and commitment to the company and employees who helped build the company.

Those who experience a successful transaction do so because they have a solid exit plan with a Strategic Succession Plan they have been implementing for several years prior to the sale of their business.

Over the years I have advised and coached a myriad of business owners, many of whom have exited their businesses. There are two companies I worked with that highlight the importance of succession planning. The contrasts between them are stark and breathtaking. One had a strategic succession plan. The other talked of having a plan, yet it was only in his head, and he failed to focus on developing his employees to prepare them for future success.

When I was a Vistage Chair, two of the business owners in our advisory group were nearing sixty years old and they started to plan for retirement, which included the sale of their businesses. Members of my Vistage group had advised both of them a succession plan would ensure they got the most value for their companies when it came time to exit.

The first owner, Dan, took the group's advice to heart. He built a robust plan driven by his management team and integrated it with his business plan on an annual basis. His goal was to have the right people in the right seats, at the right time, and doing the right things by working the plan on a continual basis.

His team was clear on the key positions in their organization, company core competencies and leadership competencies, potential versus performance, and the development planning process.

By the time Dan was ready to retire, he had developed and promoted his VP of Sales into the role of President, and he was only working one day a week. **Dan had made himself** *Replaceable*. After a year of retirement, he had two cash offers for his business with no earn out clause. Now that is what I call a successful exit! On a side note, the key employees who were part of his success all shared in the financial rewards and went on to successful careers with the acquiring company.

Now for the story of the second company: The business owner, Rick, had his company's succession plan all in his head. He never involved his management team in creating an actual plan to be implemented. Development of team members was reactive and not planned. As hard as I and the Vistage group tried to show him the risks of not having a succession plan, Rick always had something more important to do.

One Sunday, I got a call from his daughter, Tina, who was part of his management team. Rick had died the previous night from a massive heart attack. There was no person prepared to fill his shoes. No one had been developed and trained to take over as leader of the company. Rick had been the one who managed most of the key external relationships and hadn't delegated decision making power. **He made himself irreplaceable.**

Overnight the company lost its leader. Tina and the team struggled to pick up the pieces. Customers started leaving. Sadly, within eighteen months the company was shut down and the employees were on the streets looking for jobs. Rick had not embraced the importance of creating a leadership pipeline for the company he had spent his entire adult life building, and in the end there was nothing. He had left no legacy.

These two leaders chose radically different paths to succession planning. Dan chose to be proactive with developing and actively driving a succession plan, providing both a retirement income for himself as well as a legacy for his employees. Dan made succession planning a part of his annual business planning process. He had made himself *Replaceable*. Rick, on the other hand, was always too busy to focus on the development of his people. He also suffered from an underlying fear of letting go of his "baby." His whole persona was wrapped up in his company. For thirty-plus years he had put his blood, sweat, and tears into building his company, and he had no idea what the next chapter of his life would look like. He didn't have the right people in the right seats at the right time. When he tragically and suddenly died, his employees lost their jobs and the company dissolved in less than eighteen months.

Succession Planning Roadblocks

Today, 58% of all small businesses don't have a succession plan. Why do so many small businesses not have a plan? I have found three main reasons why companies don't have succession plans:

The first is because the business owner doesn't have a plan for what he will do after he exits. What on earth will he do after years of building the business? The business has defined him. Without the business, who is he? If this is you, then this isn't the book for you. If, on the other hand, you are like Dan who had made the decision to create his new life as he neared retirement, then you are ready to take on Succession Planning. For Dan, his new identity was family travel with his children and grandchildren—and getting his golf handicap down.

How do you know if you're ready to be replaceable? My experience has shown business owners are ready to become replaceable when they have a plan.

The second reason small business owners don't have a succession plan is because they don't have the systems and processes to drive a succession plan such as a development planning process, a performance management system, a core competency model, and a clear understanding of what potential means in the organization.

The third roadblock to succession planning is focus. Many small businesses are easily distracted with the daily urgencies of business and aren't disciplined to create and execute a succession plan on an ongoing basis. I have found those who create business plans using systems like Verne Harnish's Scaling Up or Gino Wickman's EOS® are more prepared to take on succession planning. Both business planning and succession planning are ongoing processes requiring discipline and an executive sponsor. In my opinion and experience, a business plan is not complete without a succession plan.

If you are among the 58% of business owners without a plan, who have a planning and execution discipline, now is the time to be proactive and create your succession plan. If you already have a succession plan, now is the time to evaluate how robust it is. **Do you have a *strategic* succession plan?** This book shows you how to develop and maintain a robust plan integrated into your existing business planning and development processes to meet the needs and resources of small and midsized companies.

Succession Planning vs Exit Planning

What exactly is succession planning? It isn't exit planning. Exit planning is the preparation for the exit of a business owner from his business. It is a comprehensive analysis identifying what impacts a business owner and his goals while also identifying the specific steps necessary to meet those goals. The goals include not only the business but also family and community. Exit planning generally spans several years prior to a business owner's planned exit.

In contrast, Succession Planning focuses on the human capital within a company. It is a systematic approach to ensuring continuity of leadership, knowledge, and expertise within an organization by developing employees and recruiting new talent to meet the future needs of the organization. **It is having the right people, in the right seats, at the right time, and doing the right things.** A true succession plan includes not only all leadership positions but also key knowledge roles such as those with technical, product, and creative expertise critical to an organization's ongoing success. **Unlike exit planning, succession planning is an ongoing process that takes place year over year.**

> Succession Planning focuses on the human capital within a company.

A well-implemented strategic succession plan is a powerful tool. It helps in assessing your talent pool to make sure employees are being developed to support the future needs of your business. For most companies, filling open leadership positions with internal candidates is an advantage because these employees have institutional knowledge of the company and appreciation of company culture that doesn't come with an external candidate.

I have found organizations will adopt one of three succession planning models:

1. The Reactive Model: Companies using the reactive model have no successors identified for key positions. They will immediately experience loss of institutional knowledge. In addition, it will take an average of twelve months to fill key positions. Even when they

find the perfect fit, 30% of the time the new employee turns over in less than eighteen months.

2. The Elementary Model: In this model, the company has one or two successors identified for each key role, but the employees aren't prepared to take on their next role. Little or no development has taken place, so the successor won't be ready for the next position when it opens up. The company lacks a planning cycle for succession planning and their identification of potential successors is not driven by data with a defined process to identify high potentials. The risk with this model is successors may leave the company because they weren't being developed, or successors have been misidentified.

3. The Strategic Model: This succession planning model will bring your company the most success. It is the only one that provides a systematic approach to ensure business continuity. A strategic plan provides your company with a talent pool of high potentials being developed to fill gaps in competencies and skills. There are clear career paths, and a long-term strategic view of talent. Only the strategic model will provide your company with the talent to support the future growth of your company and the foundation to allow you to exit or retire in your time frame and on your terms.

Dan chose to develop a Strategic Succession Plan, while Rick's plan bordered between the Reactive and Elementary models.

Is your Succession Plan strategic? Ask yourself these five questions:

1. Is the Succession Plan part of your annual planning process?

2. Is the Succession Plan updated annually?

3. Are current Key Roles, not people, identified and documented with core competency and skill requirements?

4. Have future Key Roles required to support the business plan been identified and documented with core competency and skill requirements?

5. Do you have a talent pool of Key Successors who are being developed to fill skills and competency gaps before they move into a key position?

If you can answer yes to all five questions, then you have a strategic succession plan. If you are missing at least one yes answer, then you have work to do in your succession planning process.

The contrasting stories of Dan and Rick should convince you of the need for a strategic succession plan. If not, here are some statistics to help further convince you:

- 90% of millennials will be more engaged with a clear succession plan.

- 34% of talent stays longer with a clear succession plan.

- As many as 75% of leaders will turn over in a company without a succession plan compared to 5% in companies that have one.

In addition to preparing future leaders for succession, good talent can be retained when you have a succession plan. So, let's get started!

Rapid Recall

- Make yourself replaceable so you can move on and your company can have future success.

- Exit Planning is not Succession Planning.

- Succession Planning is an integral part of your business plan.

- Only Strategic Succession Planning ensures continuity of leadership knowledge and expertise.

- A Succession Plan is not just for the executive team; it's for all key roles.

- A Succession Plan will help you to retain your high-potential employees.

CHAPTER 2
SUCCESSION PLANNING ROADMAP

"If you can't describe what you are doing as a process, you don't know what you're doing."

~ W. Edwards Deming ~

Just like a business plan, a succession plan has specific components. To create a strategic succession plan, you will complete six phases: Prepare, Identify, Analyze, Develop, Recruit, and Recognition. In the first three phases you are building your Organizational Succession Plan and in the last three phases you are executing your plan by developing your high potentials and employees in current key positions, recruiting any necessary external talent, and recognizing development progress to make job rotation and promotion decisions, and rewarding success.

Strategic Succession Planning isn't for everyone because it requires an investment of your time. For most small businesses the first three phases to build the plan will take from four to six days depending on the size of your talent pool. The execution phase of your plan will require consistent meetings and conversations with employees to track both their performance and development efforts in order to make solid decisions on promotions and job rotations to support the succession plan.

Steps to the Succession Planning Process

In Dan's case, after reviewing his business plan, organizational chart, and conducting a robust talent management discussion, it was decided his high-potential employees, with the necessary training and development, would be able to step into more senior roles at the time he needed them to be promoted. Since he didn't have to recruit for any key positions, his team had only five phases to complete in their succession planning process.

Replaceable provides you with the detailed steps and Succession Planning, SP Tools, you need to create and implement a strategic succession plan. You will find SP Tools introduced throughout the book and they can be downloaded using the QR Code provided. This chapter introduces you to the six phases of succession planning. In addition, a Succession Planning Checklist is provided to help your team keep track of your progress as you move through the process.

1. PREPARE

In the Prepare Phase of Succession Planning, your team is laying the foundation for creating and implementing your plan. There are two steps in the process: creating a team accountable for succession planning and assessing how prepared your organization is to implement a succession plan. **This phase generally takes one day with proper preparation and meeting facilitation.**

Before you start the process, it is important you have a *business plan* and an *organizational chart*. These will be crucial when you get to the **Identify phase** of the process.

Step 1: Create your succession planning team. The members of your team will include the C-Suite and leadership from HR and Talent Management at a minimum. Without the support of the C-Suite, strategic succession planning will fail. Human Resources will bring the expertise to the table when developing your core competencies, reviewing the talent pool, and assisting with development plans.

In Chapter 3, Good Teams Make It Happen, you will learn who should be on the team, how to create a team charter, and how to communicate the purpose of succession planning to your employees.

Step 2: Assess succession planning readiness. In order for a succession plan to be effectively implemented, there are many processes and organizational infrastructure that need to be in place before you proceed. If there are missing processes within your organization, they may need to be created before you start the planning process. I recommend you **reassess your readiness annually** in conjunction with your business planning. You can use an abbreviated review process by reviewing your previous year's results and making appropriate adjustments.

Chapter 4, Are You and Your Company Ready? introduces the Succession Plan Readiness Assessment where your team will assess how prepared your leadership, infrastructure, processes, and systems are to support the implementation of your plan.

2. IDENTIFY

The Identify Phase of succession planning has three steps. This is when key positions (not people), core competencies, and high potentials are identified and defined for your organization. These components will be critical in the **Analyze Phase** when you evaluate employees against core competencies and forecast employee potential. You will need your *business plan* and *organizational chart* for the Identify Phase. **Depending on how large your company is, set aside two or three days with your Succession Planning Team to complete the three steps in this phase.** If necessary, you can chunk your time down into single days. The most time-consuming portion will be Step 2, Core Competency identification.

Step 1: Identify Key Positions. These are positions critical to your current and future success. Key positions for both today and in the next three-to-five years will be determined using your strategic business plan and current organizational chart. **This step should be reassessed annually.** Reviewing your business plan is important to identifying key positions, not people, for your future success. If you have an aggressive growth plan or you plan on shifting your strategy, you will probably find key positions missing that need to be added to your organizational structure to ensure future success.

In Chapter 5, Key Positions First, you will learn about the 5 key questions to ask your team to identify the key positions in your organization today and those needed in the future to support your business plan. You will be introduced to the Key Role Identification Worksheet and the Organizational Succession Planning Roadmap.

Step 2: Identify Competencies. Competencies are observable skills, knowledge, capabilities, motivators, and/or traits needed for success in a specific job position. They define **how** goals must be accomplished, not **what** needs to be accomplished. Competencies need to be **reassessed when there are strategic changes to the organization.** Competencies will help you analyze your talent pool as discussed in Chapter 8, Where are your high potentials?

Chapter 6, Focus on the How, not the What, will guide you through the process of identifying core competencies for your company using your company values as a starting point and show you how to use the competency ladder once it has been developed.

Step 3: Define High Potential for Leadership. Unlike performance, which measures past performance, potential is a forecast of an employee's future performance. Research has shown only one in seven high-performing employees demonstrate the necessary behaviors and attitudes of a high potential. High potentials have three attributes that distinguish them from the talent pool of high performers: desire, capability, and engagement. Furthermore, potential is unique to every organization. You will need to define what potential means to your company to have your talent conversation in the Analyze Phase. Like competencies, **your definition of potential should be reassessed when there are strategic changes to the organization**.

Chapter 7, Performance is not Potential, provides you with a framework to define potential to be used in the Talent Conversation.

3. ANALYZE

The Analyze phase has two steps and is focused on evaluating your talent pool to determine your high performers and high potentials, and then assessing competency gaps for each employee. These gaps will be addressed in Chapter 10, Developing Talent for Succession. Step 1 will be completed in a group setting while Step 2 will be completed by the manager and employee with assistance from Human Resources. **This phase generally takes one or two days depending on how large your talent pool is**.

Step 1: Talent Conversation. This conversation is a process of clarifying levels of performance and potential for both key employees and the general employee pool with input from a wide group of leaders. Now that you have identified key positions, defined what potential means to your organization, and understand your core competency ladder, you can assess your employees' performance and potential. **This conversation should take place on an annual basis, at a minimum.**

In Chapter 8, Where Are Your High Potentials?, you will be introduced to the 9-Box Grid, and the Talent Pool Review Form. More importantly, you will learn how to facilitate an effective Talent Conversation to identify your rising stars and the potential positions they can be groomed for in the future.

Step 2: Analyze Competency Gaps. Determining gaps employees have to fill to be successful is a rigorous process and will be completed for each individual in your talent pool focusing attention on key employees and high potentials. Unlike previous steps, this work will be completed by the direct manager of the employee with assistance from human resources if necessary. The identified gaps will be used to create individual development plans. Analyzing gaps is an annual process to ensure development plans are updated.

Chapter 9, Competency Gap Analysis, introduces the Competency Gap Analysis Worksheet. The worksheet will help drive the development planning process in Chapter 10.

4. DEVELOP

The Develop Phase is the heart of succession planning and is the time when you and high potentials co-create individual development plans to ensure they are prepared for success in their current and future positions.

Step 1: Developing Talent. Competency and skill gaps were identified in step 2 of the Analyze Phase, Analyze Competency Gaps. Filling these gaps will require **annual development plans** for high potentials and key employees to bridge the gaps identified. Once the plans have been created, execution of the plans in a timely manner will ensure successors are prepared to take on their new roles. The types of development and level of investment will depend on the competency gaps identified, how much potential the employee has, and how fast the gap needs to be closed.

Chapter 10, Developing Talent for Succession, introduces you to the creation of a development plan, the development conversation and the various methods of development to choose.

5. RECRUIT

The Recruit phase focuses on being prepared to successfully hire external resources to fill key positions with no identified successors in your organization.

Step 1: Key Position Recruiting. Unlike other positions, when recruiting for a key position you will need to prepare for the highest degree of recruiting success. There will be key positions identified in Chapter 5 with no internal candidates identified either because there are no candidates with potential or none who will be prepared in the necessary time frame to rise into the position. Often this is a high-level position with deep functional knowledge and expertise requiring an external hire. The competency ladder built in Chapter 6 along with a consistent hiring process and hiring assessments will be the tools needed to identify the right candidate to join your team.

Chapter 11, Uncovering External Talent, covers how to attract great candidates, typical hiring mistakes, and the behavioral interviewing process. You will be introduced to the Hiring Process Checkup, Interview Process Checklist, and Shortlisting Interview Scorecard as a method to measure your organization's effectiveness in hiring employees.

Note on the Recruit Phase:

You will find the RECRUIT Phase can be skipped based on the readiness of your internal talent pool. It can also be moved to an earlier part of the process once you have completed the IDENTIFY phase of Succession Planning.

6. RECOGNIZE

There are two steps in the final Recognize phase. This phase will help you assess development progress and make decisions on promotions, which are covered in Chapter 12. In Chapter 13, you will learn about the importance of recognizing and rewarding success when your high potentials have succeeded in their development and have been promoted.

Step 1: Talent Development Monitoring and Assessment. As with any plan, development plans need to be monitored for progress with employees. Ideally the development review will be done on a quarterly basis and at a minimum twice a year. These reviews will be more efficient if your Human Resource Information System (HRIS) provides performance management and development tracking. **Monitoring should be an ongoing process.**

Employee readiness for the next role, job enrichment, or special project will be assessed by the same group involved in the Talent Pool Conversation in the Analyze Phase. Assessing readiness will become an ongoing part of future Talent Pool Conversations discussed in Chapter 8.

Chapter 12, Is there Progress?, brings together the development plan, the 9-Box Grid, the Talent Pool Conversation, and 360° assessments, and also introduces Quarterly Conversations into the development process as a means of assessing the progress of an employee's development.

Step 2: Recognition and Rewards for Success. Both the planning and execution of succession planning is a large effort by you, your team, and the employees committed to developing for future roles. It's important when your succession planning goals are met to recognize and reward those who were part of the success.

Chapter 13, Recognizing Success, provides guidance for recognizing and rewarding your team and those employees who have succeeded with their performance and development, thereby ensuring your company has a pipeline of leaders ready for the future.

Use the Succession Planning Checklist, at the end of this chapter, to keep track of your progress as you move through the six phases of Succession Planning.

Ultimately, your goal will be to have internal employees ready to move into vacant key positions or those likely to become vacant in the near term. Internal candidates provide the benefit of institutional knowledge and cultural fit. When appropriately developed, they have a higher success rate than external candidates. The strategic succession planning process ensures you have the right people, in the right seats, at the right time, and doing the right things.

Rapid Recall

- Succession Planning is an ongoing process, not a one-time event.

- Each of the six phases in succession planning play an important role in a successful implementation.

- Keep track of your progress using the Succession Planning Checklist.

- Prepare: Create your team and assess your organization's readiness.

- Identify: Identify key positions, core competencies, and define potential.

- Analyze: Review talent pool, identify high potentials, and identify competency gaps.

- Recruit: Recruit external candidates for positions with no identified internal successors.

- Develop: Create development plans for high-potential successors.

- Recognize: Monitor development plans, assess readiness for next role, and celebrate success.

- The strategic succession planning process will provide you with employees in the right seats at the right time.

SUCCESSION PLANNING CHECKLIST

To be used with Replaceable, the book

PREPARE PHASE

1. Create Succession Planning Team
   - ☐ Ask the seven questions to choose the right people for your team
   - ☐ Conduct a launch meeting and create a team charter
   - ☐ Define roles and responsibilities for team members
   - ☐ Communicate to the company your succession planning initiative

2. Assess Readiness
   - ☐ Complete the *Succession Planning Assessment* with the team, using the five questions
   - ☐ Create list of projects to support succession planning
   - ☐ Integrate projects into business plan
   - ☐ As business owner, ask the six questions to determine if you're ready to step aside

IDENTIFY PHASE

3. Key Positions
   - ☐ Create Future Organizational Chart
   - ☐ Complete the *Key Role Identification Worksheet*
   - ☐ On *Organizational Succession Planning Roadmap,* fill in Key Position title and Held By rows in each column
   - ☐ Update Key Position Job Descriptions

4. Competencies
   - ☐ Identify employee behaviors supporting company values
   - ☐ Identify leadership behaviors driving organizational success
   - ☐ Create two competency ladders, one for all employees and another for leaders
   - ☐ Update job profiles by incorporating competencies into job profiles
   - ☐ Review future strategy to determine additional competencies to support your company's future success
   - ☐ Rate employees on each competency and behavior using your competency ladders

5. Potential

- [ ] Conduct career conversations
- [ ] Define potential using the attributes: aspiration, capability, and engagement
- [ ] Complete the *High Potential Identification Worksheet*
- [ ] Train managers on how to identify high potentials
- [ ] Communicate to your high potentials why they have been chosen and your expectations of them.

ANALYZE PHASE

6. Assess Your Talent Pool

- [ ] Conduct a Talent Conversation
- [ ] Complete the *Talent Pool Review*
- [ ] Place each employee in one of the nine boxes on the *9-Box Grid*
- [ ] Complete the *Organizational Succession Planning Roadmap* started in step 3.

7. Analyze Competency Gaps

- [ ] Revisit your two competency ladders
- [ ] Complete the *Employee Competency Assessment*
- [ ] Conduct 360° Assessments if appropriate
- [ ] Interview Feedback partners
- [ ] Conduct Performance Conversations

DEVELOP PHASE

8. Development Plans

- [ ] Complete the *12-month Development Plan* for employees
- [ ] Conduct a Development Conversation for each employee
- [ ] Ask the four questions when deciding on methods of development
- [ ] Train managers on how to coach employees
- [ ] Track employee development progress

RECRUIT PHASE

9. Hiring Great People

- [ ] Complete *Hiring Checkup List*
- [ ] Identify key positions which have no internal successors identified using your completed *Organization Succession Planning Roadmap*
- [ ] Attract quality candidates by using the three techniques
- [ ] Use the *Interview Process Checklist* before interviews to ensure consistency
- [ ] Avoid the eight common hiring mistakes
- [ ] Embrace the Behavioral Interview process
- [ ] Create behavioral interview questions to consistently ask candidates
- [ ] Use the *Shortlisting Interview Score Card* to assist in hiring decisions

RECOGNIZE PHASE

10. Measuring Progress

- [ ] Move candidates up the *Organizational Succession Planning Roadmap* as they develop
- [ ] Measure development based on success metrics in development plan
- [ ] Hold Bi-annual Talent Pool Conversations and replot employees on the 9-Box Grid as they develop
- [ ] Have quarterly conversations with employees to review development progress
- [ ] Use succession planning metrics to measure your planning effectiveness.
- [ ] Measure implementation of each phase of the process using the *Succession Planning Checklist*

11. Recognizing Success

- [ ] Align your rewards and recognition program to your values and culture
- [ ] Recognize both individual and team success
- [ ] Customize rewards and recognition based on employees wants and needs by asking the five questions
- [ ] Evaluate your program by asking the seven questions

INTRODUCTION TO PREPARE PHASE

Phase 1 of Succession Planning, PREPARE, includes two steps: Creating your Succession Planning Team, and Assessing your Readiness as an organization to execute a succession plan. These steps create a solid foundation before heading into subsequent phases of Succession Planning.

In this phase, we will discuss how and why a succession planning team is critical to successful plan implementation, how to put a team together, and how to identify potential gaps your organization may have that can block the road to success.

SP Tool(s) introduced during the PREPARE phase:

- Succession Planning Readiness Assessment

Question: Are you, your team, and your organization ready to take on the development of a strategic succession plan and successfully implement it as part of an ongoing practice?

Warning! If you are a business owner, you need to prepare yourself for what life looks like after your business. *You* could turn out to be the biggest roadblock to implementing a strategic succession plan. Put your personal plan in place to ensure succession planning success.

CHAPTER 3
GOOD TEAMS MAKE IT HAPPEN: THE SUCCESSION PLANNING TEAM

"The strength of the team is each individual member. The strength of each member is the team."

~ Phil Jackson, NBA Coach ~

Remember Dan's story of succession planning success? When Dan made the decision, he wanted to retire at age sixty and had three years to get his team ready for his exit. His goal was to sell the business and leave his employees with a piece of the financial proceeds and future employment. He had a clear goal. After his exit decision, he assembled his succession planning team, the first step in the succession planning process. His team was committed to the successful development and implementation of the company's succession plan.

Remember, succession planning is a process not a one-time event. When you decide you are personally ready as business owner/CEO to take on succession planning as discussed in Chapter 1, implementation is ongoing and dynamic. Assessment of talent will continue as high potentials and key employees are developed, redeployed, and promoted. Key positions may also change as your strategy changes.

In the PREPARE Phase, the first step in the Succession Planning Process is to bring your team together. Your job is to prepare your management team for what lies ahead. Your team's goal is to develop a strategic succession plan and review it annually to keep it alive and healthy. As CEO, President, or Business Owner you need to convey the importance of this initiative to your team. All members of the team need to embrace the mission of succession planning and be fully engaged.

Your team members will have control over and/or influence on the steps within the Succession Planning process. Ultimately, the CEO will be accountable for the plan because without CEO support and accountability, succession planning is unsustainable. While HR should be involved, they should not be the ones accountable for the plan. Otherwise, succession planning becomes an exercise of filling out forms and documenting opinions of **high potentials.**

High Potential: A high performer demonstrating a high capacity to grow and succeed more quickly and effectively than other high performers and demonstrates behaviors supporting their company's values and culture.

In Dan's case, his company was private, with just under 100 employees. He had an executive team of five: CEO/President, VP of Sales, VP of Client Services, VP SW Support, and VP Finance, all with direct reports, and an additional four managers. He decided to include all leaders with direct reports and the HR Manager who did not have any direct reports for a total of ten team members.

Dan made his decisions about who to invite to join the team by asking himself a series of questions to identify the ideal members. Here are the questions he asked himself:

1. Who is knowledgeable about the business plan?

2. What functions need to be represented on the team to support the planning process?

3. Who is knowledgeable about our core and leadership **competencies**?

4. How much influence do they have within the organization?

5. Do they have the time to commit to the process?

6. How well do they communicate across the organization?

7. What role will they play on the team?

Competency: A competency represents a broad combination of the knowledge, skills, and personal attributes that can predict high performance in companies. They can be observed and measured and contribute to employee performance and company success.

Question 3 is important and often misunderstood by small businesses. In my experience, few small businesses with less than 100 employees are knowledgeable about core and leadership competencies. Having a basic competency ladder is critical not only to assess high potentials but also for use in the hiring process. We will explore competency ladders and how to build them later in Chapter 6, Focus on the How, not the What.

The size of your team will depend on the size of your company. Larger companies will have a larger team. For smaller companies, the team will, at a minimum, include the CEO and an HR/Talent Management leader as part of the team. If your company is a partnership, such as accounting and law firms, the team can get quite large. For these companies, equity partners are generally given the opportunity to be on the team before non-equity partners in order to keep the numbers manageable.

With the succession planning team formed, it is time to communicate to your team the importance succession planning is to the company's future success.

When Dan delivered his message, it was clear and concise with a sense of urgency. He had set a three-year exit timeline and knew implementing a succession plan to have people ready to rise and take on expanded roles was going to take time. The process the team was preparing to embark on was going to benefit the entire organization. He needed their full commitment for the plan to be successful.

Once you have identified the members of the team, it's time to have a launch meeting. This meeting is designed to clarify roles and responsibilities and create a team charter. The charter document serves as the compass for the team. It will include the team mission, scope of operations, objectives, metrics, and time frame. And it will be reviewed when there are changes to the team members and/or annually.

As you define team roles and responsibilities, refer back to the questions asked when you were forming your team. Pay special attention to questions four through six. Some roles may require more time and influence than others. It's important you, the business owner or president, be sensitive to the time required for developing and implementing the plan for individual members of your team. As sponsor of the succession planning initiative, your role is not to manage the day-to-day development and deployment of the succession plan, but to ensure proper resources are available to promote the succession plan, and to hold overall accountability for the success of the plan.

Communicating the Succession Planning Process to the Company

After the team launch, it's imperative to make an announcement to all employees the team is committed to an organizational succession plan to ensure employees are being developed to meet the future needs of the company. This communication will come directly from the business owner or president of the company.

The most effective way to communicate the upcoming succession planning process companywide is in person or by way of a webcast. It will give employees the opportunity to ask you questions regarding the process. And when it comes from you, the business owner, it demonstrates to employees succession planning is a high priority to you and the company. It also shows them there is a consistent process for identifying potential leaders and developing employees to their full potential.

Without a consistent process, employees will become disengaged and think employees having closer relationships to their managers will have an advantage in being promoted. You want employees to feel confident the system of identifying high potentials is equitable and fair.

This communication will be especially impactful to Millennials in the workforce. It's estimated over 90% of Millennials would have a higher level of engagement if they knew there was a clear succession plan in place for them.

In Chapter 7 we will discuss how to communicate succession plans specifically to high potentials.

With your team formed, roles assigned, and a charter created, it's time to evaluate your organization's readiness to develop and support a succession plan, Step 2 of the PREPARE phase.

Rapid Recall

- Sponsorship of the Succession Planning Process is the CEO's responsibility.

- Ask the seven questions to choose the right people for the Succession Planning Team.

- Knowledge of the business plan and talent management systems is needed on the team.

- Create a team charter, the true north for your team.

- Communicate the succession planning process to the organization to increase engagement.

CHAPTER 4
ARE YOU AND YOUR COMPANY READY? SUCCESSION PLANNING READINESS

"Preparedness is the key to success and victory."
~ Douglas MacArthur ~

When was the last time you decided to try a new recipe or learn a new sport or hobby? You didn't start down the new path without making sure you had the equipment and supplies required to be successful. Succession planning is similar. It requires preparation. Your company needs to have the right infrastructure in place to support the implementation of a plan, otherwise your plan is at risk of not being implemented and properly maintained. Your managers also need to be knowledgeable about succession planning and developing employees.

A succession plan requires key systems and processes, including a performance management system, defined career paths, a development planning process, rewards and recognition systems, definition of high potential, a core competency model, an assessment process to support core competencies, and a system to track the development progress of successors and other high potentials.

As a team you need to evaluate these components and determine what systems and processes are missing or incomplete that need to be put in place before you start your succession planning. Some gaps can be filled as you plan while others should be in place before you start the process, such as a performance management system, career paths, and a development planning system.

Succession Planning Readiness Assessment

To assess your readiness, you will need the SP *Succession Planning Readiness Assessment*. The assessment is organized into organizational infrastructure, key roles, competency model, assessment process, development process, and implementation of succession plan.

When Dan brought his team together, they used the Readiness Assessment. Each member rated the statements on the Succession Planning Readiness Assessment by their level of agreement. There were a number of statements about which people disagreed, so they drilled down to what evidence they had to support their level of agreement/disagreement. This is an important step to the planning process. You want to make sure team members are in alignment and there is consensus of how prepared your organization is to take on a succession plan. This process can be lengthy, and it is often more efficient to have an outside facilitator help the team come to consensus on each of the statements.

You can find an example of the *Succession Planning Readiness Assessment* at the end of this chapter or online at www.executive-velocity.com. Notice the example has four columns: a statement, a rating, evidence supporting the rating, and a priority. Prior to bringing your team together, I recommend each member rate the statements on a scale of 1–4 where 1=Disagree,

2=Partially Disagree, 3=Partially Agree, and 4=Agree. Then members should identify the metrics, documents, and/or processes supporting their ratings. The priority column will be completed by the Succession Planning Team as one of their first action items.

Once all team members have completed the assessment, the team will meet and identify those items you agree on and those you need to come to consensus on. Discuss items with less than a 4 rating and prioritize the items you want to elevate to a 4 rating. If there are a significant number of 1s and 2s, then focus on items rated a 2 or 3 you can move up to a 4 with a project plan.

Here are five questions to help you with prioritization:

1. What items are low-hanging fruit that can be quick wins?

2. What items might not be appropriate due to the size of your organization?

3. What roadblocks are in the way?

4. Are there related items that can be incorporated into one project or a current project?

5. What items can be delayed?

The result of this meeting will be a list of projects to include in your business plan for the following year to support your succession planning process. Remember, you don't have to get all the components in place before you start the planning process—that's why you prioritized the list. A good example is management training that should occur closer to when management needs to use the newly acquired skills. In fact, it is preferable to provide training at a point when employees can apply their new knowledge shortly after receiving it. Research shows 70% of new information is forgotten within twenty-four hours, regardless of how important it is to us. The ultimate goal of learning is to be able to effectively apply the new knowledge, and it's more difficult to apply the longer it can't be put it into practice.

In contrast to Dan's team, Rick and his team actually reviewed their readiness for succession planning and identified projects they needed in their business plan to support succession planning. Unfortunately, the team failed to hold themselves accountable and most of the projects were never completed. Part of this failure was Rick, who was sponsoring the succession plan. He had too many other priorities and succession planning kept falling to the bottom of the list. This is a good reminder the leader responsible for the succession plan needs to be fully committed and have the bandwidth to drive the process forward. For Rick and his company, because the projects were not completed, a good performance management system wasn't available for the company to track performance and development of employees, a critical component of succession planning.

For Dan and his team, there were several areas managers needed training in such as identifying, developing, and coaching high potentials. They decided to include all managers in Phase 3, Step 1 of the planning process, the Talent Pool Conversation. Including all managers in the talent conversation provided managers with the necessary knowledge to identify high potentials on their team. To address training for developing and coaching high potentials, this training became part of the managers' development plans.

You now have your list of projects and incorporated the high priority ones into your business plan. The team can begin to develop your organizational succession plan. Ultimately the more prepared you are, the more successful the implementation of your succession plan will be.

Owner Readiness

While the purpose of this book is to layout the process of developing and executing a succession plan, I would be remiss not to remind the reader of one roadblock to successful execution of a plan: the business owner. The majority of business owners I've worked with haven't taken time to plan what they will do after their successor takes the reins. A mere 4% of business owners have a formal, written plan for life after business. This low figure shouldn't surprise anyone who knows a business owner. They have put their life into the business and put hobbies and other outside interests on the back burner for years.

Succession planning readiness includes the readiness of the business owner. If you are the business owner, a best practice is to start focusing on what your life purpose will look like in the future and creating a transition plan allowing you to step back from your business incrementally. Some common activities I have seen business owners get involved with as they started stepping back include travel, reconnecting with friends, revisiting old hobbies, learning new skills, obtaining board positions with non-profits, and exercising regularly. Ultimately, your job is to become **replaceable** and to let those who you have developed step up to greater responsibilities.

How ready are you as a business owner to start the succession planning process? Start by asking yourself these six questions:

1. Do I have positive thoughts when I think of retirement or exiting the business?

2. Do I have a plan for the first six months after exiting the business?

3. Can I envision what my ideal week would look like without work?

4. Can I immediately think of two activities I would do if I had more personal time?

5. Do I have friends who have successfully transitioned out of their business?

6. Do I have a support system outside of my work?

If you are unable to answer yes to at least five of the questions, then you aren't prepared to exit your business. Remember, exiting and succession planning aren't synonymous. Succession planning is making sure you have a leadership pipeline for the key roles in your company at all times. But if you are close to exiting your business, then you need to be emotionally prepared to let go and move on. Like Dan, you need to be okay with becoming **replaceable**.

Dan really embraced the idea of becoming replaceable because he had gone through the step of planning for his retirement. As his successor became more prepared to take on the role of President, Dan became more confident he could spend less time at the office. The process was gradual over three years. He started taking more trips with his extended family, his golf game improved, and he was giving his time and expertise to several non-profits. When the time came to sell the business, Dan was working less than a day a week and had made himself **replaceable**.

Rick, on the other hand, really struggled with the idea of letting go, especially with his long-term clients. We worked hard on executing a plan for him to become replaceable, yet the plan was never fully implemented as he kept getting pulled back into client activities. An underlying reason was he was enabling leaders to pull him back into client issues and he loved working with clients. It was a major blind spot for him. He wanted to feel needed, and he wasn't committed to designing his life after exiting his company. So instead of coaching his leaders to deal with future client issues, he was ultimately inviting them to come to him to solve client problems.

If you are following Dan's lead, you now have your succession planning team together and you have measured your organization's readiness to take on developing and implementing a plan. Your team has been empowered to take on the identified projects and you will keep them accountable to their commitments. The Prepare Phase has been completed. Congratulations! You are ready to move onto Phase 2: Identify.

Rapid Recall

- Organizational infrastructure needed to implement a succession plan includes a performance management system, defined career paths, core competency model, development planning process, and rewards and recognition systems.

- Prioritize projects to support your succession planning process and build into your annual business plan.

- Business Owners need to prepare their lives for "after the business."

SUCCESSION PLANNING ASSESSMENT

The cornerstone of a company's success is their talent. Having the right people in the right seat, at the right time, doing the right things, is the goal of a solid succession plan. Succession Planning is a systematic approach to ensuring continuity of leadership, knowledge, and expertise within an organization.

A true succession plan includes not only leadership positions but key knowledge roles such as those with technical, product, and creative expertise critical to an organization's ongoing success.

How prepared is your organization to create and implement a solid succession plan? This assessment is designed to measure your readiness to create and implement a succession plan. When completed you will have the necessary information to move forward with a successful plan.

Directions:

1. For each statement rate your organization on a scale of 1–4

   1. You disagree
   2. You partially disagree; the company has this partially in place with no plans to complete
   3. You partially agree; the company has this partially in place and is currently working on completing
   4. You agree

2. In the next column, document the metrics and/or processes your company has in place to support your ratings.

3. Have other members of your succession planning team do the same analysis and then meet to determine which statements you are in agreement and what specific items you need to come to consensus. Once you agree on the ratings of each item, it's time to prioritize.

4. Discuss items with less than a 4 rating and prioritize the items you want to elevate to a 4 rating. Use the column to the far right to prioritize statements as a team. Assign each statement a priority of 1–3.

- 1 = needs to be completed before starting
- 2 = can be completed within 6 months
- 3 = can be completed after 6 months

Here are some suggestions on prioritizing:

- If there is a significant number of 1s and 2s then focus on items rated a 2 or 3 that, with a plan you, can move to a 4.
- What items are low-hanging fruit that can be quick wins?
- What items might not be appropriate due to the size of your organization?
- What roadblocks are in the way?
- Are there items that are related that can be incorporated into one project or a current project?

Organizational Infrastructure

Role	Rating 1–4	What evidence exists to support rating?	Priority 1–4
A succession planning team is in place with specific roles and responsibilities.			
A performance management system is consistently used for all employees.			
A current, documented organizational chart exists.			
All job descriptions are current with core competencies included.			
The hiring process is consistently attracting top candidates to fill key positions.			
Managers have been trained and empowered to effectively deliver performance feedback.			
Career paths are defined.			
The development planning process is defined and implemented for all employees annually at a minimum.			
Managers have been trained on creating and monitoring development plans.			

Organizational Key Roles

Role	Rating 1-4	What evidence exists to support rating?	Priority 1-4
A future organizational chart exists to align with business strategy.			
Key roles have been identified by evaluating current and future skills needed for the business strategy.			
Career Paths for key roles have been defined.			
Managers are trained on how to identify, develop, and coach high potentials.			
Roles and responsibilities of succession planning are clear and there are C-Suite members actively engaged in the process.			

The Competency Ladder

Role	Rating 1-4	What evidence exists to support rating?	Priority 1-4
The business has defined core competencies supporting their values and specific competencies for leadership and subject matter experts.			
The key role profiles focus on a few key competencies.			
Competencies are defined in terms used within the business.			
Core competencies supporting company values have been communicated to all employees.			
The competencies are reviewed and updated on an annual basis to align with business strategy.			

Assessment Process

Role	Rating 1-4	What evidence exists to support rating?	Priority 1-4
Company key roles have been analyzed to determine required knowledge, experience, and competencies; both required and desired.			
Assessments are based on the core competencies as defined in the job descriptions.			
Potential has been defined and is understood by those with direct reports.			
Talent Conversations take place on an annual basis to track key employee and high potential progress.			
The 9 Box Grid is understood and used to evaluate employees' potential and performance.			
The assessment process is viewed by employees as fair, objective, and without bias.			
The assessment processes are integrated into the succession planning process.			

Development Process

Role	Rating 1-4	What evidence exists to support rating?	Priority 1-4
High potentials receive support from managers in preparing their development plans to align with their realistic career aspirations.			
Managers have been trained on creating and monitoring development plans.			
Types of development are aligned with the competencies associated with key roles.			
A variety of development options are available including stretch assignments, action learning sets, coaching, mentoring, and formal training.			
Managers have been trained on conducting career conversations.			
There are quarterly reviews and follow-up on personal development plans to measure progress.			
The organization monitors progress of development against key positions.			

Implementation of Succession Plan

Role	Rating 1-4	What evidence exists to support rating?	Priority 1-4
There is a system to collect data so that the succession planning can be monitored and measured.			
Those not in line for key roles are developed, as well, and career paths have been communicated.			
Plans are in place to mitigate against the risks of not meeting the expectations of those in the talent pool.			
A communication plan for those identified as 'successors' is in place.			
A well-defined process has been implemented to track and manage, and assess all employees, especially the talent pool of successors.			

INTRODUCTION TO IDENTIFY PHASE

There are three crucial steps in the IDENTIFY Phase. The three steps are: Identifying your company's key roles, determining your core competencies, and defining what potential looks like in your organization so you can identify your potential future leaders.

Key roles are not key people. Key roles are the positions critical to your strategic plan and future success. Once you have identified your core competencies, you can use them for both performance management and hiring. And unlike performance, potential is predicting future success, not measuring past performance. You will need to understand what potential looks like when we introduce the 9-Box Grid in the ANALYZE phase.

SP Tool(s) introduced in the IDENTIFY phase:

- Key Role Identification Worksheet

- Organizational Succession Planning Roadmap

- High Potential Identification Worksheet

Question: Do you know how to **consistently** identify your future leaders? Who will be able to succeed to higher level positions **fully prepared** to take on their new roles?

Warning! This phase is time consuming and may take up to four days to complete the steps of identifying key roles, defining core competencies, and defining potential. The good news is once you have completed these steps you only need to review the information annually and make necessary revisions, decreasing the investment in your team's time significantly.

CHAPTER 5
KEY POSITIONS FIRST: WHAT POSITIONS ARE CRITICAL TO YOUR COMPANY'S SUCCESS?

"…it's surprising how few companies systematically identify their strategically important

A *positions*—and *then* focus on the A players who should fill them."

~ Mark Huselid, Richard Beatty, and Brian Becker ~

You have completed *Phase 1: Prepare* by assembling your succession planning team and identifying any gaps in your processes and infrastructure that will hinder you from successfully implementing your plan. You've prioritized the gaps and the most important items have been included as projects in your annual business plan.

Your team can now move into the second phase, *Identify*. In this phase your team will review your business plan and organizational chart to identify positions critical to your company's future, identify the core competencies of your company and its leadership, and define what high potential is to your company.

The first step in the Identify Phase is identifying the key positions in your company today and the key positions needed to support your future strategy.

You will need the following documents and tools:

- Business Plan, Vision/Traction Organizer ™ (EOS®) or One Page Strategic Plan™ (Rockefeller Habits)

- Organizational Chart or Accountability Chart™ (EOS®)

- *SP Key Role Identification Worksheet*

- *SP Organizational Succession Planning Roadmap*

Positions or People?

What do you assess first—key positions or key people? When it comes to succession planning you need to start with key positions. Employees can come and go but positions are more stable. A company will always need a position to oversee finances or sales, but the person in that position can change over time. What positions are critical to your success today and in the future? This is where many smaller companies go astray. They focus on the people in the positions first instead of the positions.

Like many companies, Dan and his team had always focused on key employees. Retaining and developing them was always a topic of discussion as well as a concern. As they were educated on strategic succession planning, they realized it was important to analyze the organization's needs first, both for today and the future.

Your Business Plan and Organizational Chart or EOS®
Accountability Chart™ will be used as reference points during
the process of identifying key positions. These documents will
help you identify your key positions today and in the future.
This is not the time to talk about the people in the key positions
but to simply identify the critical positions for organizational
success. Which roles will have the greatest impact on your
company's performance and which ones will be the most difficult to replace? A discussion of the people in these positions
will take place during the Talent Conversation in Chapter 8.

Using your Business Plan and current Organizational Chart,
adjust your organizational chart to support your future business
strategy. What positions will you need to add? What current
positions will need to be upgraded, redesigned, combined, or
eliminated?

When identifying your key positions, your team should ask
these five questions:

1. What level of risk on business success is associated
   with the position if it should become vacant?

2. How many unique skills or knowledge does the position require?

3. How many internal candidates could be backfills for
   the position?

4. How likely are you to find an external candidate to
   backfill the position?

5. How quickly will you need a successor for the
   position?

When Dan and his team started the process of identifying
their organization's key positions, they enlisted the help of all

the managers in the company. As a team, they knew the managers could provide more insight about positions lower in the company than they had as a smaller group with less exposure to the positions below them. As a group they evaluated each position, from senior leadership to receptionist, using the questions above. To organize and prioritize the positions, they used the *SP Key Role Identification Worksheet* to score each position in the organization. You will find the worksheet at the end of this chapter.

The result was a complete list of all positions with assigned scores for each one. The higher the number, the more likely the position was key to the organization's success. Dan's succession planning team decided a key position would be one which needed to be filled in the next twelve months and had a number assigned to it of twenty-eight or greater. This list would be the starting point of their succession plan for the year.

It will be up to your team to determine what scores are required for a position to be designated a key position. And remember, there could be positions that don't exist now but will be critical to your company's future success. These positions as well as existing ones that meet your key position score will be documented on the first row of the *SP Organizational Succession Planning Roadmap*, found at the end of this chapter. And the names of any employees currently in those positions can be entered into the "Held by" row. You will be filling in the potential successor names on this chart when you get to Chapter 8.

Update Key Position Job Descriptions

Smaller companies often have outdated job descriptions that are generally updated only when they are looking to hire a new employee. Having a current job description for key positions will be important when you get to Phase 3: *Analyze*. You will be referencing the job description to analyze employees currently in the role against an accurate and updated job description.

Once you have identified your organization's key positions, you will review the job descriptions for each position or create one if it's a new position. Your Core Competencies will be incorporated into each job description which we will be discussing in the next Chapter.

Rapid Recall

- Documents needed include Business Plan, Organizational Chart.

- Succession Planning Tools Introduced: Key Role Identification Worksheet, Organizational Succession Planning Roadmap.

- Start with key positions, not key people. Positions are more evergreen and don't change as much as people.

- Ask the five questions to identify key positions in your organization.

- Review job descriptions of key positions and update if needed.

KEY ROLE IDENTIFICATION

Directions

This worksheet is designed to be used by a company's Succession Planning Team. The Succession Planning Team should consist of the Executive Team and a representative from Human Resources. You will need your Strategic Plan and Organizational Chart to reference during Key Role Identification. Once you have successfully identified your Key Roles, you can start the process of evaluating employees currently in the roles and create development plans for them.

For companies with less than fifty employees

The Succession Planning Team should list all current positions having direct reports, and positions reporting directly to the CEO/President regardless of direct reports. List any additional leadership positions and/or positions requiring specialized knowledge which will be added to your organization based on your business plan.

Then rate each position for the seven criteria. Ratings should be 1 = none, 2 = minor, 3 = neutral, 4 = moderate, 5 = major. The total score will provide you with a ranking of key roles. The higher the rating the more key the position is to your company's success.

For companies greater than fifty employees

Follow the steps above and then add this next step: Managers of individual contributors should evaluate each direct report position using the same criteria and then review their results with the Succession Planning team. The list from the Succession Planning team and the list(s) from managers are combined to create one list to rank all positions.

All companies should review job descriptions to ensure they are current and include core competencies. Current job descriptions will be necessary to define gaps in competencies, skills, and knowledge that will be addressed in individual development plans.

Current Positions	Impact on today's business 1–5	Impact on Future Business 1–5	Scarcity of external resources 1–5	# of Qualified HIPOs* 0 = 2 or more 1 = only 1 5 - none	HIPOs are ready for succession 0 = ready now 3 = ready in in <18 mos. 5 = ready in in >18 mos.	Specialized Knowledge difficult to replace 1–5	Risk of losing current employee 1–5	Total Score 5–35	Job Description Reviewed Y/N
Future Positions									

*High Potential Employee (HIPO)

ORGANIZATIONAL SUCCESSION PLANNING ROADMAP

Date: _____

Key Position Title:					
Held By:					

Candidates Ready Today					

Near-Term Candidates (Ready in 1–3 Years)					

Future Candidates (Ready in 5+ Years)					

Using This Template:

1. List the leadership and key positions within your organization and the present holder of the role.

2. Identify the various individuals within your organization that could readily step into the given leadership roles immediately should a vacancy arise.

3. Using the 9-Box Grid, identify those high potentials who could step into a given leadership role soon (1–3 years) after some development, mentoring, and coaching.

4. Using the 9-Box Grid, identify high potentials who would be long-term successors to leadership positions (5+ years) following training and development activities.

5. Individuals may be listed in multiple boxes, based on their career interests and goals.

6. Review this list annually; consult the list as vacancies and changes in your organization occur.

CHAPTER 6
FOCUS ON THE HOW, NOT THE WHAT: AN INTRODUCTION TO CORE COMPETENCIES

"To be a manager requires more than a title, a big office, and other symbols of rank.

It requires competence and performance of a high order."

~ Peter Drucker ~

You and your team have arrived at one of the most important steps in succession planning and overall talent management—defining your Core Competencies.

> Competency: A 'blend' of knowledge, skills, experience, behaviors, and values. When put in action, an individual with the right "blend" performs their responsibilities in a way that gets results.

When Dan started down the path of Succession Planning and integrated it into his annual planning process, he completed the *SP Succession Planning Assessment* to identify which key components were missing or incomplete to support his plan. For his company and many others of similar size, the **Competency Model or Ladder** was a missing piece of the puzzle.

What makes a competency model so important in the succession planning process? Core competencies predict future high performance in companies. They can be observed and measured, and they contribute to employee performance and company success.

A competency is simply a 'blend' of knowledge, skills, experience, behaviors, and values. When put in action, an individual with the right "blend" performs their responsibilities in a way that gets results.

Competencies are generally built from one job level to another. An example would be communications. An entry level position will require a lower level of communication skills than a manager or executive to be effective. Competencies help employees focus their behaviors on what is important to and valued by your organization and are the foundation of employee development and success. They provide a common way to select, measure, and develop talent.

There are many benefits to using a competency framework, such as more effective hiring, evaluating performance, identifying competency gaps for development plans, and better succession planning. When developed and used effectively, they help employees develop and grow incrementally. And with succession planning, they are critical for ensuring you have the right people, in the right seats, at the right time, and doing the right things.

Creating your Core Competency Ladder

You will need the following documents to create your Competency Ladder:

Global List of Competencies
Key Role Job Descriptions

Most large companies create and implement a core competency model, detailing each competency and the various proficiency levels of a competency required for each position. Here's an example of competency levels:

Fundamental Awareness, Novice, Intermediate, Advanced, and Expert

Additionally, each job position will have its own competency model. If you are a company of fifty employees, you could have upwards of forty models depending on your organizational chart. As a smaller company, I don't recommend implementing an entire competency model because the process is rigorous and expensive, and once you have a model it, takes time to update and train managers on how to use it effectively.

Instead, I recommend you stick to this abridged approach that creates two broad **Competency Ladders**, one for all employees and one for leaders. These ladders are developed by identifying behaviors supporting your company values, strategy, leadership, and specific skills for a position. The behaviors will then be organized into broad competencies.

When developing his Competency Ladder, Dan assembled a team of leaders from across the company to get a diverse representation. They started with a pre-set list of global competencies and then customized the list to their needs based on their values, strategy, and leadership. An example of the list of competencies Dan's team used is at the end of this chapter.

Values First

Company values are your company's DNA. They are the beliefs and principles driving your decision-making and actions for your business, and your values impact the experience your employees, customers, and partners have with your company. Values-based competencies will be the benchmark for future hires as well as existing employee assessment, development, and deployment.

I have rarely worked with a company who didn't have documented core values, yet many hadn't taken the next step to define the behaviors and actions supporting those values. I have even found this to be true with companies using the EOS® Entrepreneurial Operating System. While the EOS® People Analyzer™ helps you assess whether an employee is the right person in the right seat, it doesn't take the important step of helping to define the specific behaviors and actions that demonstrate a value.

Values are abstract while behaviors can be observed and explained with more clarity. The first step to defining core competencies is to determine the specific actions and behaviors which demonstrate your company values.

> Values are abstract while behaviors can be observed and explained with more clarity.

Dan's company had their values, but they hadn't determined the specific employee behaviors they would observe to validate employees were living company values. Their values included the following:

- Integrity
- Working Together
- Excellence
- Innovation

You can see from their example how values are abstract, and it isn't until behaviors are linked to a specific value that you understand exactly what the company is looking for from their employees.

Dan and his executive team met to develop a list of behaviors for each value. During their discussion they asked themselves three questions to define the specific behaviors the company was looking for from all their employees:

1. Which employee(s) do you think of when we talk about a specific value?

2. What actions does the employee specifically display consistently that proves they are living a value?

3. Which of these actions are the most important to our company and its success?

In addition to their discussion, they referred back to the Global List of Competencies, found in the Appendix of this book, to see if they wanted to add any additional behaviors required for their strategic direction.

After answering the three questions and reviewing the list of competencies, they had the following list of specific behaviors aligned with their values:

- **Integrity:** Take responsibility for actions, do what you say, communicate openly.

- **Working Together:** Working and supporting other team members, building two-way relationships with employees and customers, understand and respect other people's priorities.

- **Excellence:** Go the extra mile for customers and employees, deliver consistent results, continuously develop skills and knowledge.

- **Innovation:** Curious, challenges status quo, applies new ideas to drive positive change, emphasizes speed and agility.

Since values are core to a company's culture, these behaviors became part of each job profile. They were also used as the basis of behavioral interviews for their future hires. We will discuss how to create a behavioral interviewing process in Chapter 11, Hiring Success for Key Positions.

Leadership Competencies

Unlike values competencies, which will be part of every job profile, leadership competencies are unique to positions managing departments, projects, and other employees. These positions require additional characteristics, skills, and behaviors to drive results and be successful. So, in addition to the values-based competencies, you will need to determine competencies critical to leadership success in your organization.

A common way to organize leadership competencies is into five distinct areas: Managing Self, Managing Projects, Managing People, Managing Programs, and Leading Organizations.

In today's rapidly changing environment some of the common leadership competencies I see in companies include the following:

- **Leading Change:** Anticipates and implements needed change while meeting the organization's short-term goals (leading organizations).

- **Partnering:** Works effectively across departments and with external organizations (managing programs and projects).

- **People:** Attracts, develops, and retains talent for the organization and inspires teams to achieve goals (managing people).

- **Influence:** Quickly earns trust, creates win-win situations, gets others to buy into a vision (managing people).

- **Acting with Empathy and Compassion:** Displays the ability to understand the situations and points of view of others and communicates this understanding back to the other person (managing self).

- **Strategic Thinking:** Understands how company strategy impacts team hiring and development, presents new value-added ideas and plans about how to implement them based on knowledge and external trends (leading organizations).

While these are some common leadership competencies, you will need to create your own unique set of competencies that set your leadership apart and support your future goals and strategy. For a small monthly fee, I recommend visiting the website www.leadershipcompetencieslibrary.com as it provides you access to a comprehensive list of 120 leadership competencies.

Organizational Competencies vs Employee Competencies

It is important to note only employee core competencies are the components to a competency model. They should not be confused with the core competencies of a business. Organizational competencies are the competitive advantage(s) a business holds over its competitors and are not part of an employee competency model. An organizational competency is a specific process, intellectual property, asset, or capability in which a company excels. Since they are a competitive advantage, these competencies are focused on the services or products from which your company's customers benefit and can't be acquired easily by your competitors.

An organizational competency is a specific process, intellectual property, asset or capability in which a company excels.

While it is important to understand your company's core competencies, for succession planning the focus is on your human capital.

Future Strategy

Your business strategy will shift as your company grows, and as your strategy changes so will your Competency Ladder. The competencies necessary to help realize your future objectives may be different from the ones you have identified for today.

In Dan's example, innovation was a value that had been added as a result of a significant shift in strategy from services to technology-based services. If his team had an existing Competency Ladder, they would have needed to adjust the model to address this shift in strategy. No longer were they focused on efficiency but growth and innovation. It is important to review your Competency Ladder annually to determine if you need to make adjustments to either your core or leadership competencies.

Update Job Descriptions

Once the core and leadership competencies have been identified, you will review the job descriptions of those key positions identified in Chapter 5 and incorporate the competencies into the job descriptions.

Using the Competency Ladder

You will now have two competency lists, one core competency list all employees will be measured on, and another list specifically for leadership competencies.

Below are Dan's two lists. You will notice there is a rating column. The ratings are meant to simplify the assessment process for employees. An employee with a "3" rating demonstrates the behavior more than 70% of the time, a "2" rating demonstrates the behavior 40-70% of the time, and a "1"rating means the behavior is demonstrated less than 40% of the time.

Core Competency	Behavior/Skill/Knowledge	Rating 1, 2, 3
Integrity	Takes responsibility for actions	
	Does what they say	
	Communicates openly	
Working Together	Works with and supports other team members to drive results	
	Builds two-way relationships with employees and customers	
	Understands and respects other people's priorities	
Excellence	Delivers consistent results	
	Goes the extra mile for customers and employees	
	Continuously develops skills and knowledge	
Innovation	Curious	
	Challenges status quo	
	Applies new ideas to drive positive change	
	Emphasizes speed and agility	

Leadership Competency	Behavior/Skill/Knowledge	Rating 1, 2, 3
People Developer	Implements ways to build positive morale	
	Gives people timely feedback	

	Coaches people to reach their full potential	
Strategic Thinking	Foresees long-term implications of proposed positions	
	Identifies and considers emerging opportunities and risks	
	Exercises sound judgment in new situations	
Team Orientated	Holds people accountable for results	
	Makes good hiring decisions	
	Effectively deals with conflict	

Use this method to analyze each employee. The results will be important when you get to Chapter 8, in which your team assesses your talent pool to identify your high potentials.

Rapid Recall

- Core competencies of employees represent a broader combination of the knowledge, skills, and personal attributes that predict high performance in companies.

- Create two broad competency lists—one for all employees and one for leaders.

- These models are developed by identifying behaviors that support your company values, your strategy, and leadership.

- Values-based competencies will be the benchmark for future hires as well as employee assessment, development, and deployment.

- Leadership competencies are unique to those positions managing departments, projects, and other employees.

- Six common leadership competencies include Change Leadership, Partnering, People, Influence, Acting with Empathy and Compassion, and Strategic Thinking.

- Your business strategy will shift as your company grows, and as your strategy changes so will your competency ladder.

- Incorporate competencies into all job descriptions but most importantly for your key roles.

CHAPTER 7

PERFORMANCE IS NOT POTENTIAL: HOW TO FORECAST FUTURE PERFORMANCE

"A company's greatest asset is its high-potential leaders."
~ Ram Charan, Author, *The Leadership Pipeline* ~

Performance is not Potential

During a coaching conversation, my client, Suzanne, Vice President of a Telecommunications firm, was struggling with the performance of Saul, an employee who had recently been promoted. I inquired how she made the decision to promote Saul. She quickly responded that Saul had always been a high performer and a good team player. He had supported others on the team when they were behind on their projects or had trouble with technology. I responded, "Sounds like Saul is a high performer who likes to help others, correct?" Suzanne replied, "That's exactly right. And leaders need to be willing to help others around them." She was right; leaders do need to be willing to help others, but leadership is much more than helping.

Since her organization hadn't started a succession planning process, she hadn't identified core competencies. So, we decided to define the competencies needed to define a high potential in Suzanne's organization. We came up with a list of five competencies potential leaders needed to display in order to be considered high potentials: adaptability (being quick to adapt to changes), decisiveness (ability to make the hard decisions), curiosity (inquiring and learning), coaching (developing others), and strategic thinking (forward, big-picture thinking).

When we compared this list of leadership competencies to Saul, he was weak in two of the competencies: adaptability and strategic thinking. As a high performer in the world of technology, Saul was used to projects that had direction, yet he wasn't the one who initiated the projects based on strategic needs he identified. Also, prior to his promotion, he hadn't been exposed to situations where he needed to inspire others to change to a different direction. In short, he was at a disadvantage when he was promoted.

> Performance measures past performance while potential attempts to predict future performance.

Small business owners generally have an idea of what potential looks like, yet it's all in their heads. It's the old "I'll know it when I see it" syndrome. *Defining the behaviors and actions that demonstrate potential is more important than you might think. When they are documented, they can be communicated to employees, so everyone understands how potential is being measured. Doing this will bring transparency into the process of promotions and job rotations.* When you have the Talent

Conversation in Chapter 8, everyone will know how to measure the potential of employees.

One of the biggest mistakes I see small businesses make is confusing high performance for high potential. Performance measures past performance while potential attempts to predict future performance. Did you notice the word *attempts*? This is because predicting the future is not easy. It requires a keen understanding of what potential looks like for your company and having the methods to measure potential, and managers trained to observe for potential in employees.

According to the Corporate Executive Board, only one in seven high performers demonstrate the traits of high potentials. High potentials not only are high performers, but they also show a high capacity to grow and succeed more quickly and effectively than other high performers. Moreover, they demonstrate the behaviors that support their company's values and culture.

There is also the good but not stellar performer who may have potential to do great things for your company but is overlooked because they aren't in the right seat. You could be passing over employees who may have a positive future impact on your company because you aren't clear on the difference between potential and performance.

> High potentials are high performers who demonstrate a high capacity to grow and succeed more quickly than their peers.

As a succession planning team, one of the most important tasks you will have to do is defining what potential looks like in your organization. Once you have defined it, you need to be able to measure potential for those in your talent pool.

Dan's story of succession planning took the familiar path of most small businesses. He had elevated a high-performing Client Service Rep into a supervisor position prior to defining potential. The promotion was less than a success. In the end, he had to demote the person, which caused the employee to ultimately leave the company. He didn't want to repeat this mistake.

So, he and his team created a definition of what potential looked like for their company. This was one of the gaps they had identified when they performed the Succession Planning Readiness Assessment mentioned in Chapter 4, and it was a gap that needed to be filled before launching their succession plan.

Career Conversations

Before defining potential, you will need to engage in a career conversation with your high-performing employees if you haven't already done so.

You will be surprised to find there are some high performers who are perfectly happy in their current role and don't have the desire to climb the corporate ladder. These individuals may have made this decision because of their personal situation or professional interests. Subject matter experts are a group of employees who often opt out of leadership positions. They like being experts and moving into leadership would take them away from their craft such as science, engineering, programming, accounting, and so on.

Career conversations are designed to uncover an employee's long term professional goals and help employee engagement and retention.

You can determine if a high performer has the desire to take on a greater role in your company by having a Career Conversation with them. While Dan and his team had annual career conversations, they weren't structured and consistent across the organization. Each manager had their own process—a common problem found in smaller companies. Inconsistency in talent management and human resource processes can be especially problematic because it creates the perception of inequity among employees. I have found this inconsistency quite often with smaller companies because their human resource department is generally understaffed and focused on the tactical rather than the strategic.

> **"To understand a person's growth trajectory, it's important to have career conversations in which you get to know each of your direct reports better, learn what their aspirations are, and plan how to help them achieve those dreams"**
>
> **~ Kim Scott, Author, *Radical Candor* ~**

Career conversations are often overlooked by leaders. I recommend these conversations occur at least once a year, although twice a year is ideal as personal situations may change and impact an employee's professional goals. All employees should have a career conversation, not just the high performers. When career conversations uncover an employee's long-term goals, managers can help align the employee's current tasks and responsibilities to their future aspirations and in turn increase employee retention and engagement. In short, career conversations are a tool for employee engagement.

If you haven't started the process, your initial conversation will be to understand the employee's desire to take on added scope and responsibilities. Get curious and learn about your employees' values, gifts, interests, and skills. You will need to understand the whole person, not just the person's performance. Create a list of questions to help the employee self-reflect on where they want to be in the future. There may be points at which they won't have an immediate answer, or they may feel uncomfortable with the questions. After all, many employees have never had a deep career conversation with their manager. If this should occur, don't try and rescue them! Get comfortable with the silence. If you feel the silence becoming awkward, just say "take your time." This gives them permission to further self-reflect and not feel rushed.

Here are some sample questions for a Career Conversation:

- Looking back on your professional life, what event or person had the most impact on your success and why?

- What do you love doing most in your work?

- What challenges you at work?

- What would you like to learn more about?

- If you could design your career exactly how you'd like it, where would you be working, what kind of people would you be working with, and what value would you be providing to the company?

- If you were at the pinnacle of your career and fully engaged, what would you be doing?

After your initial career conversation, you should know whether the employee has a desire for taking on an expanded role.

With this additional information, you can discuss options for the employee to consider in a follow-up conversation once you have completed the talent pool assessment outlined in chapter 8. While a move upwards is often thought of first for high potentials, there are other options that can help an employee advance their career. These options include a lateral move into a different department to provide exposure to new business/company knowledge, enriching a current job with more chances to learn and develop, and realigning a position by offloading less complex tasks and adding more valuable ones .

Remember, high potentials will often want to have an option of moving up. If your company is not going to be able to provide this option in the short term, then you need to provide other interesting options for career growth.

Career conversation tips:

- All employees deserve career conversations, not just high performers.

- Have a list of questions to ask each employee to get them to self-reflect about their life journey, key life events, their values, their long-term goals, what brings them joy and angst, and so on.

- Use this information to help with employee development plans and determining future potential in the company.

Defining Potential

How do you start to define potential? Many of the small business owners I have worked with generally have a good idea of what potential leaders will be demonstrating in their actions and behaviors. Research has shown that a high potential has three attributes that distinguish them from the talent pool of high performers: aspiration, capability, and engagement.

Now that you've had the career conversation to understand the career goals of your employees, you need to evaluate the three attributes distinguishing high potentials from high performers.

The *SP High Potential Identification Worksheet* will help you to assess the three attributes described below. You can find the worksheet at the end of this chapter.

1. Aspiration: High Potentials drive to rise to more senior roles in the company

Once you have determined your high performers have the 'want' during the career conversation, you need to determine if they have the motivation and behaviors to support their aspiration.

It's one thing to want to move up in the organization, it's another to have the motivation and drive to succeed.

Motivation

There are **five motivational factors** highly correlated to the drive for advancement: immersion, activity, power, interest, and autonomy.

Remember those career options discussed in the career conversation? Apply these questions to the employee's choice of career options as well as their recent choices to determine their level of motivation:

Immersion: Do they seek out positions requiring a personal commitment greater than the average company commitment?

Activity: Do they prefer environments that are fast-paced and multi-tasking?

Political Power: Do they desire opportunities to influence and shape decisions on how things are executed?

Interest: Do they look for positions and assignments providing variety, intellectual stimulation, and a challenge?

Autonomy: Are they attracted to roles allowing them some autonomy in how they execute their responsibilities and deliver results?

2. Capability of High Potentials

Capability is measured by those skills needed for future success as well as behaviors supporting your company's leadership competencies such as learning agility, adapting to change, and self-management. The performance review process can assist in measuring employee skill levels. Capability also includes the core competencies identified in Chapter 6.

3. High Potential Engagement

Engagement is the level of commitment an employee has and is measured by the following four elements:

1. **Emotional Commitment:** The employee values and enjoys the company. They believe in the mission, vision, and long-term success of the company.

2. **Rational Commitment:** The employee believes it is in their best interest to stay employed by the company.

3. **Discretionary Effort:** The employee consistently goes the extra mile for the company.

4. **Intent to Stay:** The employee has a high level of commitment to stay with the company.

Employees who score high in all three attributes of aspiration, capability, and engagement have the highest potential to rise into key leadership positions while employees high in one or two attributes can be very valuable team members but do not have as high a potential to take on higher levels of responsibility.

**For smaller companies, I recommend adopting an abbreviated version of identifying potential. They should focus on two criteria for potential: 1) Potential to advance in the same functional area either through scope of work or at a higher level in the organization; and 2) Potential to take on different organizational roles in different departments.

Training Managers to Identify High Potentials

One of the statements on the *Succession Planning Assessment* is "Managers are trained on how to identify, develop, and coach high potentials." If your company is smaller, training managers to identify high potentials is probably a lower priority. If the succession planning team is knowledgeable in identifying high potentials and know how to use the 9-Box Grid, training of other managers is a development opportunity but not a requirement.

Communicating to High Potentials

Communicating to those identified as high potentials is an important part of this step in the process. Done well, it can provide benefits related to retention, motivation, and engagement of your most talented employees. Letting employees know they are in the high potential pool signals you value their contributions to the company and want to invest in their future. Delivered well, the message shows them what their future looks like if they continue employment with your company.

When communicating to a high potential, make sure to share the criteria they met to be in the high potential pool. You should also share what expectations you and the company have for the employee moving forward including future development and career opportunities. Ask them what they will need for support during the development process and share the support you can offer. This is the time to review their development plan with them, which is covered in Chapter 10. Be careful to manage employee expectations. While their future performance and commitment to their development will be important to their professional opportunities in the future, it doesn't guarantee a promotion or change in their job.

Understanding what potential is in your organization takes time in defining potential using the *SP High Potential Identification Worksheet*, and then it takes practice by managers to have career conversations, observe high potential behaviors, and share their observations during Talent Conversations so your organization can make solid talent decisions to support succession planning.

Rapid Recall

- Performance looks at the past while potential predicts the future.

- Career conversations will increase retention and engagement for all employees.

- Define what potential looks for your company.

- High potentials can be measured by aspiration, capability, and engagement.

- Complete the *SP High Potential Identification Worksheet*.

- Communicate to high potentials to increase retention, motivation, and engagement.

HIGH POTENTIAL IDENTIFICATION WORKSHEET

Only one in seven high performers demonstrate the traits of high potentials. High potentials not only are high performers, but also show a high capacity to grow and succeed more quickly and effectively than other high performers.

A high potential has two attributes that distinguish them from the talent pool of high performers: aspiration and engagement. In addition to these attributes, they will demonstrate behaviors supporting your company values and core competencies and have the ability (skill sets) to be successful in future leadership roles.

Use this worksheet to measure the potential your employees have. Once you have rated all your employees, then you can map each employee on the 9-Box Grid using their performance ratings and potential ratings. In Section 1 you will measure aspiration and engagement. A YES answer is one point, and a NO answer is zero points. An employee can have a maximum of eleven points.

In Section 2 you measure ability. Ability includes the core competencies and skill sets identified for an employee's job profile. An employee with a 1 rating demonstrates the behavior less than 40% of the time, a 2 rating demonstrates the behavior 40-70% of the time, and a 3 demonstrates the behavior greater than 70% of the time.

Your team will need to determine how many points are required to qualify as a high and medium potential employee.

SECTION 1

ASPIRATION AND ENGAGEMENT	Employee 1	Employee 2	Employee 3	Employee 4	Employee 5
Do they seek out positions requiring a personal commitment greater than the average company commitment?					
Do they prefer environments that are fast-paced and multi-tasking?					
Do they desire opportunities to influence and shape decisions and how things are executed?					
Do they look for positions and assignments that provide variety and intellectual stimulation?					
Are they attracted to roles that allow them a degree of autonomy in how they execute their responsibilities?					
Does the employee value and enjoy the company?					
Does the employee believe in the mission and vision of the company?					
Does the employee believe that it is in their best interest to stay employed by the company?					
Does the employee consistently go the extra mile for the company?					
Does the employee have a high level of willingness to stay with the company?					
TOTAL POINTS SECTION 1					

SECTION 2

ABILITY	Employee 1	Employee 2	Employee 3	Employee 4	Employee 5
Core Competencies*					
Leadership Competencies*					
Specific Skill Set*					
TOTAL POINTS SECTION 2					
TOTAL POINTS					

*See definitions on the following page.

Core Competencies: Core competencies of employees represent a broader combination of the knowledge, skills, and personal attributes that can predict high performance in companies. Core competencies are behaviors that support your company values, your strategy, and leadership. They can be observed and measured and contribute to employee performance and company success.

Leadership Competencies: Unlike core competencies, which will be part of every job profile, leadership competencies are unique to those positions that manage departments, projects, and other employees. These positions require additional characteristics, skills, and behaviors to drive results and to be successful. Examples of leadership competencies include: achieving results, continuous learning, leading change, strategic thinking, and emotional intelligence.

Skill Sets: A skill set is a combination of knowledge and abilities that are needed to perform a specific job. Some skill sets are specific to a job, such as an accountant. An accountant will need specific skills related to accounting to be successful in an accounting position. Other skill sets are not job-specific such as written and verbal communications. Depending on the types of skills, they can either be obtained through training and/or experiences.

INTRODUCTION TO ANALYZE PHASE

This phase has two steps. The first step is the Talent Conversation, which is completed in a group setting and is designed to gain a broad range of insights from leaders other than an employee's manager who have had experience working with specific employees. The conversation is designed to gather information so employees can be assigned to one of the boxes in the 9-Box Grid.

The second step is completed by the employee's manager to determine missing elements from an employee's skills and competencies that need to be developed before elevating them into a more senior position. As their manager you will revisit the Competency Ladder in Chapter 6 and the *Organizational Succession Planning Roadmap* to complete the *Employee Competency Assessment.*

SP Tool(s) introduced during the ANALYZE phase:

- 9-Box Grid

- Employee Competency Assessment

Question: Who are the leaders who have potential to rise to the next level? What competency gaps need to be developed for them to be successful in their next position identified in the Organizational Succession Planning Roadmap?

Warning! Understanding and identifying high potentials is one of the most misunderstood parts of succession planning. Don't rush through this part of the process of defining what a high potential is for your organization. Also, assessing key employees against your criteria will ensure you have the right employees being prepared for succession.

CHAPTER 8

WHERE ARE YOUR HIGH POTENTIALS? ASSESSING YOUR TALENT POOL

"The real value is the discussion, not the rit-
ualistic review of data and stale facts.

Encourage different views and options to talent considerations."

~ Kevin Wilde, Author, *Dancing with the Talent Stars* ~

You and your team have moved into Phase 3 of Succession Planning, which is *Analyze.* The Analyze phase is when your management team discusses the performance and potential of employees and identifies competency and skill gaps employees need to fill in order to grow into their full potential.

The first step in analyzing your company's talent is to engage in a rigorous Talent Conversation.

Dan and his team came together to have their Talent Conversation for the first time. Unlike the succession planning team, the team who participated in the talent conversation was broader and included managers who could share their observations of employees' behavior and performance. These managers understood the Competency Ladder developed in Chapter 6 as well as the company's definition of high potential. Since the first step in the conversation is discussing employee performance, team members brought employee **job descriptions** and **performance reviews** with them. At the time, they did not have an integrated Human Resource Information System (HRIS) to house job descriptions, employee performance, and development plans, so they were working from several stand-alone documents.

The Talent Conversation: A time when leaders gather to share their experiences and opinions of employees. Information from the conversation will be used as part of process of identifying high performers and high potentials.

Do you remember back in Chapter 3 when you assessed your company's readiness to create and implement a succession plan? This was the point Dan realized his company didn't have all the systems in place to execute all the components of a succession plan such as development plans. His team made the decision to move forward with succession planning while addressing the operational gaps in performance management and development in parallel with succession planning.

Note: The larger the company, the more important it will be to have an integrated HRIS. This system will help with reviewing relevant talent pool data prior to the talent discussion. The talent discussion is where different opinions and experiences with employees can be explored and information gathered. A performance management system can't capture this level of nuanced information.

In addition to job descriptions and performance measurements/reviews, there are three tools you will need during your talent discussion: *SP The Talent Pool Review Form, 9-Box Grid Template,* and the *Organizational Succession Planning Roadmap.*

Talent Pool Review Form

The *SP Talent Pool Review Form* will help you document each employee's performance, potential, and readiness for new responsibilities. The information on the *SP Talent Pool Review Form* will be used to complete the *SP 9-Box Grid.* The form can be found at the end of the chapter.

9-Box Grid

The *SP 9-Box Grid* is a tool to help facilitate annual conversations around performance management, employee development, and succession planning. The grid is an important tool for the Talent Pool Conversation. The original 9-box matrix was developed by McKinsey back in the 1970s to help GE prioritize investments. At some point, HR took the model and adjusted it for use in talent management.

Using the *SP 9-Box Grid* allows participants in the talent conversation to plot employees based on performance and potential. Employees are mapped against two axes: current performance and future potential. The grid provides an important framework to manage all employees consistently throughout an organization. Each box provides developmental and performance management scenarios you can use as a starting point for individual development plans.

For smaller companies, generally less than fifty employees, the Succession Planning Team will assign employees into one of the nine boxes on the grid using the definition of high potential created in Chapter 8, along with performance review data. Larger companies will train managers on how to use the *SP 9-Box Grid* and then they will present the results to the Succession Planning Team. This is a collaborative process, and your managers will benefit by hearing alternative views of employees. A variety of views will provide a more objective and less biased assessment of employees in your talent pool.

Once the *SP 9-Box Grid* is complete, you will revisit the *SP Organizational Succession Planning Roadmap* used in Chapter 5 to identify your organization's key positions and current employees in those positions. In Chapter 5 you partially completed the chart. Now you can complete your *SP Organizational Succession Planning Roadmap* with potential successors by key position and development time required. The information in this chart will be used in Chapter 10 to create development plans for your employees.

Organizational Succession Planning Roadmap

The roadmap shows you which candidates you have identified to be developed for a key position and the time required to develop the candidate for success in their future role. The information gathered using the *SP 9 Box Grid* will be critical to completing the *SP Organizational Succession Planning Roadmap*, introduced in Chapter 5. It will also be updated twice a year as described in Chapter 12.

Talent Conversations

Done correctly, the Talent Conversation allows managers to probe a wide range of leadership criteria and obtain a more balanced and complete view about employees' talent. Engaging a wider range of opinions will decrease the halo effect and mitigate other biases. When you include multiple opinions and data, the Talent Conversation will help your organization avoid making bad promotion decisions. Talent conversations will take place twice a year to ensure development progress is updated as discussed in Chapter 13.

These conversations include the employee's manager as well as other managers who have observed the employee's behavior and performance directly over time and during different circumstances.

To properly assess a high potential, during the talent conversation managers need to consider a full complement of leadership criteria, including leadership competencies and other skills important to predicting potential. Final decisions should be made by integrating the various views and opinions from those who have managed and collaborated with the employee.

Because the Talent Conversation was new to Dan's company and the results of the conversation would impact key talent in the organization, Dan hired an outside facilitator for this step in the Succession Planning process. Someone from the outside can bring fresh perspectives and ask difficult questions of the team, and a facilitator will shift the dynamics of the conversation to create a more neutral and unbiased interchange of opinions and ideas. I highly recommend companies engage a facilitator during the Talent Conversation.

During the conversation, everyone in the room who has interacted with the employee has the opportunity to share their experiences relating back to the Competency Ladder and job description of the employee.

Example of a Talent Discussion Agenda

- CEO Introduces the purpose of the meeting and how the results will impact the company strategically.

- HR Reviews Competency Ladder.

- HR Reviews the definition of potential in the company.

- Discuss each employee with the direct manager starting with employee performance and moving to potential. At the conclusion of each conversation the employee will be added to the Talent Pool Review Form, documenting levels of performance and potential.

- Each employee is then mapped onto the 9-Box Grid.

- Time is spent discussing potential future positions into which the high potentials might fit.

Communicating to High Potentials Revisited

At the end of Chapter 7, I explained how important it is to communicate in the right ways to high potentials in order to show them they are valued, they have a path forward, what that path looks like, and asking them what support they think they'll need. This is also a good time to assign a coach/mentor to your high potentials.

Now that your high potential employees know their future opportunities, you need to put a development plan together to help them meet their goals. Before creating the plan, however, a competency gap analysis needs to be performed.

Using the SP Tools: *Talent Review Form, 9-Box Grid,* and *Organizational Succession Planning Roadmap* in your Talent Conversations will provide you and your team with a consistent method of identifying your high potentials. Understanding who has the potential to succeed into key positions will increase the odds of your succession plan being a success.

Rapid Recall

- Participants in the Talent Conversation should be able to share actual observations of employees' behaviors and results.

- Talent conversations provide a wider set of data and observations than a traditional performance review.

- *SP Talent Pool Review Form* documents each employee's performance, potential, and readiness for new responsibilities.

- *SP 9-Box Grid* allows participants in the talent conversation to plot employees based on performance and potential.

- A talent discussion brings together your Competency Ladder, definition of Potential, and actual performance to plot performance and potential on the grid.

Instructions:

Performance level — WHAT the employee does and HOW they do it. Rate each employee relative to the following criteria:

I. Weak performer
II. Solid performer
III. Strong performer

Ultimate potential level — The job level the individual is capable of attaining, provided continued performance and development (under best possible conditions). Consider raw capability, motivation, and desire to succeed, and engagement to the group or organization.

I. Current role only or possible bad fit
II. Good fit at current level, lateral move, or upward one level
III. Upward mobility more than one level

Readiness — Consider the individual's learning needs and potential when making this judgment.

I. Needs greater than twelve months to develop to next move
II. Should develop in current role for more than twelve months before next move
III. Can take next development step within next twelve months

Talent Pool Review

Direct report name	Performance level	Potential level	Readiness		
			I	II	III
1	Sample: John Smith	III	III		✓	
2						
3						
4						
5						
6						
7						
8						

9-Box Grid Template

Instructions:

Here you will take the information from the Talent Pool Review form and plot employee performance against potential. Working collaboratively, arrange every employee into one of nine types across a vertical and horizontal axis, based on three levels of performance and three of potential.

The 9-Box Grid guide on the next page provides more insight and recommended actions.

Potential: The ability to assume increasingly broad or complex accountabilities as business needs change during the next 12-18 months.

Enigma	Growth Employee	Star
Develop	Stretch/Develop	Stretch
Assess	Core Employee	High Impact Contributor
Observe	Develop	Stretch/Develop
Bad Hire	Effective Employee	Trusted Professional
Observe/Exit	Observe	Develop
Does not meet expectations	Meets expectations	Exceeds expectations

Performance (based on current job): The extent to which the individual:

a) Delivers business/functional results   b) Demonstrates core competencies   c) Acts in the spirit of the companies values

9-Box Grid Guide

Potential:
The ability to assume increasingly broad or complex accountabilities as business needs change during the next 12-18 months.

An individual who has recently been promoted and hasn't had the opportunity to demonstrate higher performance. Focus on coaching and a solid development plan. An individual who has been in this role for some time, there may be a serious issue (derailer). **Develop**	A valuable asset for the future. There is still room for maximizing performance in current role; potential may not be fully realized yet. Focus on increasing performance contribution to high, after which greater challenge and/or broader scope are likely. **Stretch/develop**	Has mastered current role and is ready (and anticipating) a new challenge. Next steps are to provide greater scale and/or scope or a new assignment, which will stretch them in a significant way or will provide new or missing skills. Retention is critical. These are future leaders of the company. **Stretch**
Shows some potential but performance is considered low. Focus on reasons for low performance and actions to improve it. If there isn't an improvement, potential should be reassessed and a performance improvement plan put in place. **Observe**	Has potential for increased accountabilities and is meeting current performance expectations. Development focus: Increase performance contribution to "high" with further assessment of potential growth. **Develop**	Is exceeding performance expectations and is a good candidate for growth and development. Employee development should focus on specific gaps – i.e., what is needed to broaden or move to the next level of responsibility. **Stretch/develop**
Not meeting performance expectations and demonstrates limited potential. Focus should be on significant performance improvement or finding a more suitable role (internal or external). **Observe/exit**	Consistent contributor but shows limited potential. Focus on maximizing performance while assessing future potential and/or a more suitable role. May need a plan for a successor. In some cases, if performance declines or is blocked, retention may be reviewed. **Observe**	A strong performer but unlikely to move to a higher-level role. Engagement will be important for continued motivation and retention. May be of real value for developing others. Professional, business, or content experts may fall into this box. **Develop**

| Does not meet expectations | Meets expectations | Exceeds expectations |

Performance (based on current job): The extent to which the individual:

a) Delivers business/functional results   b) Demonstrates core competencies   c) Acts in the spirit of the company's values

CHAPTER 9

COMPETENCY GAP ANALYSIS: WHAT'S MISSING?

"Good and solid analysis and a formal way of looking at a problem are the core ingredients of good decisions."

~ Colin Powell ~

Up until this point, most of your succession planning work has been completed by the Succession Planning Team or your extended management team during the Talent Conversation. The work moving forward is focused on the manager, and the high potential employee.

The second step in the Analyze Phase is a competency gap analysis to identify what is missing from an employee's set of skills and competencies for them to be successful. Completing this analysis provides you with the necessary goals for a development plan to be built in the next chapter. Remember, managers need to be trained in how to complete this step for gap analysis to be effective.

When Dan and his team arrived at this step of analyzing skills and competency gaps, they had a clear understanding of what competencies their leaders and key employees needed to be successful. They had also identified employees who had potential to take on greater responsibilities in the future with appropriate training and development.

Identifying competency gaps is critical to creating meaningful development plans to prepare your leaders for future responsibilities. Dan's leadership team was focused on having the right people, in the right place, at the right time, and doing the right things. Follow Dan and his team's steps in analyzing employee gaps.

First, you will revisit your *Competency Ladder* developed back in Chapter 6. At the end of Chapter 6 there was an example of how Dan used his competency ladder to assess his key employees and high potentials against the competencies. Information from the competency ladder has all the core and leadership competencies a position requires to use in the *SP Employee Competency Assessment*.

Employee Competency Assessment

The *SP Employee Competency Assessment* is the tool you will use to identify the development priorities for employees over the next twelve months. The information in the assessment will be used in the next chapter to create the employee's development plan. The goal is to prepare your key employees and high potentials for their next role and/or provide them with training to be successful in their current position. You will find this assessment at the end of the chapter.

To complete the *SP Employee Competency Assessment* input the competencies and skills required for the employee to be successful in Column 1, which will come from the *Competency Ladder* in Chapter 6. Then rate the employee on each competency/skill using the scale of 1–4 in column 2 described on the assessment. The ratings 1–3 align with the *Competency Ladder* in Chapter 6 with the additional rating of 4, which is for competencies and skills demonstrated over 95% of the time.

The next step is determining the rating level the employee needs to be successful in their current position OR be prepared for the next position documented on your *SP Organizational Succession Planning Roadmap*. Enter your rating in column 3. Then prioritize the specific gap based on the following:

1. How critical it is for success in the current position.

2. Taking on a broader role.

3. A non-critical development opportunity and enter in column.

4. Finally, in column 5 you will identify the top three development opportunities based on the results in column 4.

This prioritization will help you determine the gaps to be addressed in the next twelve months and will be used in Chapter 10.

Measuring Existing Competency Levels

How do you measure existing competency levels for column 2? There are three ways of measurement: 360° Assessments, Feedback Partners, and Performance Reviews. The more methods you use, the less biased the rating will be.

360° Assessments

The 360° assessment uses collected anonymous feedback from direct reports, managers, peers, and sometimes business partners, as well as a self-assessment, to identify areas where employees can strengthen their skills in order to progress effectively. It is designed to measure the core and leadership competencies associated with a person's position.

---

360 assessments are used to get candid, anonymous feedback on skills and behaviors of an employee from employees at different levels in an organization.

The assessment is not an evaluation of performance, but rather constructive feedback for developmental purposes. For the sake of reliable answers, confidentiality is extremely important in this process.

In the 360° assessment, you and the employee will want to ensure you have a group of people with a diverse range of experiences with the employee. Some will be direct reports, commenting on the management and leadership style of the employee. Some will be peers who understand the employee's position and work with the employee on projects and initiatives, and some will be internal collaborators and may even include external professional contacts. Finally, the employee's managers and skip reports will provide their assessments, describing what they believe the employee needs to achieve and fulfill their potential. It is important these raters understand they are not performing an evaluation; they are instead providing feedback meant to help the employee succeed.

Feedback Partner Interviews

In smaller companies of less than fifty employees, a 360° assessment may not be practical. When getting feedback from a 360° assessment, you want at least ten people to provide anonymous feedback. When you have a small pool of people to choose from, anonymity becomes difficult.

Instead of using a 360° assessment, feedback partners can be valuable in identifying competency and skills gaps. When feedback partners have experience with the employee's work and understand what core competencies the employee should be displaying, their input is immensely beneficial. Feedback partners can provide insights into performance and behaviors you may not have had the opportunity to observe.

For Dan's team, they chose to use feedback partners. While they had eighty employees, they decided a 360° assessment was not a process they were prepared to support in the next several years. Instead, I was asked to interview feedback partners of the key employees and high potentials they wanted assessed for competency and skill gaps. Having an outside resource conduct interviews with feedback partners is less intimidating to those being interviewed. Their specific responses will remain anonymous. And the interview often uncovers information a 360° may not reveal because a third party can ask probing questions to follow up on initial responses. If you choose to use an internal resource, your human resources manager trained in conducting these types of interviews is a good choice.

Performance Conversations

Performance reviews serve as another way to identify current skills and competency gaps. However, they shouldn't be used exclusively as a method to assess for development opportunities but to supplement a 360° assessment or feedback partner interviews. If you are using EOS®, then the 5-5-5™ will serve as the performance review.

Gone are the days of the annual performance review; performance reviews should be an ongoing and frequent discipline between a manager and an employee. They are especially important for the success of your succession plan.

Instead, I like to refer to these reviews as Performance Conversations. These conversations should take place at least quarterly but ideally on a monthly basis. In today's business environment, change happens quicker than it did twenty years ago, and as a manager you need to stay abreast of your employees' progress. Monthly performance conversations will provide the opportunity for you to coach and mentor your employee to make more timely adjustments. They will also ensure fewer surprises during a performance conversation.

I recommend using an automated platform like GetLighthouse (www.getlighthouse.com) to document accomplishments and future commitments resulting from your conversations.

With the three techniques of 360° assessments, feedback partners, and performance conversations, you can complete the *SP Employee Competency Assessment* and identify the development priorities for the next twelve months. You can now move into the Development Phase confident you are focusing on the development of your employees to make them and your company successful. The Development Phase places you, the manager, in the roles of coach, mentor, and advocate.

Rapid Recall

- The employee's manager will be responsible for identifying "what's missing" with an employee's competencies.

- The Employee Competency Assessment is a critical tool in preparing for employee development. It helps prioritize development goals for the next 12 months.

- Current competency ratings can be determined using three techniques- 360° Assessments, Feedback Partner input, and Performance Conversations.

- 360° assessments provide confidential feedback on an employee's competencies from peers, direct reports, managers, and the employee.

- Through individual interviews, Feedback Partners understand what an employee's competency levels are from direct interaction with the employee.

- Performance conversations need to be on a regular basis, monthly is best. And outcomes of these performance conversations should be documented.

EMPLOYEE COMPETENCY ASSESSMENT

Manager: .... Employee: .... Job Position: .... Date: ....

Before creating a development plan, an assessment of key competencies needs to take place. This worksheet will help you to identify an employee's development priorities for the next twelve months. Review this with the employee during your quarterly development conversations and integrate into the employee's development plan.

Competencies: The list of competencies will come from the employee's job description.

Competency/Skills Ratings:
1. NOT DEVELOPED: Demonstrates less than 40% of the time
2. DEVELOPING: Demonstrates 40-70% of the time.
3. FUNCTIONAL: Demonstrates more than 70% of the time
4. EXEMPLARY: Demonstrates Best Practices on a consistent basis

Competency Goal: The level needed to be met in the next twelve months as described above.

Development Priority:
1. Critical to success in current position
2. Critical to taking on broader role
3. Development Opportunity

Required Development: Those top three competencies with the highest development priorities

Competency-Behavior/Skill	Current Competency Rating 1--4	12-month Competency Goal 1--4	Development Priority 1--3	Required Development in next 12 months Y/N

INTRODUCTION TO THE DEVELOPMENT PHASE

Phase Four is dedicated to developing your high potentials identified during your Talent Conversation using the *SP High Potential Identification Worksheet*. You will be working with your high potential employee to co-create a twelve-month development plan to ensure they are prepared for the next position identified for them in the *SP Organizational Succession Planning Roadmap*.

The goal of the plan is to fill the competency gaps you identified your high potential has in the *SP Employee Competency Assessment* and to develop the competencies and skills in the time frame needed for them to step up into a more senior role.

SP Tool introduced in the DEVELOPMENT phase:

- 12-Month Development Plan

Question: Do all your employees, not just your high potentials, have a development plan tying back to your organizational goals as well as one that meets the personal and professional goals of your employee?

Warning! While creating a plan is a collaboration between you and your employee, and an annual event, having ongoing development conversations to monitor progress is a commitment of time for both you and the employee as discussed in Chapter 12.

CHAPTER 10

RIGHT PERSON, RIGHT SEAT, RIGHT TIME: DEVELOPING TALENT FOR SUCCESSION

"The growth and development of people is the highest calling of leadership."

~ Harvey S. Firestone ~

When Dan and his team arrived at this succession planning step, they had already been developing their employees because they understood development is an investment in their employees as well as their organization's long-term success. What they were missing was a strategic link between employee development and succession planning. Once they understood the competency gaps for both their current employees residing in key positions as well as potential successors to those key positions, they crafted development plans to build their strategic leadership pipeline.

While we have focused on high potentials and succession planning, the content in this chapter can be used for all employees, not just those who have been identified as potential successors to your key positions.

Organizations who are committed to developing their entire workforce enjoy a number of benefits such as reduced employee turnover, increased employee productivity, increased employee engagement, and decreased internal talent shortages.

It's the responsibility of every leader to engage in their employees' development. Without leadership engagement your company is not fully committed to developing your talent. No longer is money a competitive advantage—*talent* is the advantage.

> **"If your actions create a legacy that inspires others to dream more, learn more, do more and become more, then you are an excellent leader"**
>
> **~ Dolly Parton ~**

In this chapter you are introduced to the SP *12-Month Development Plan*. To create the plan you will need the following supporting documents: Job Description, Performance Conversation Documentation, and *SP Employee Competency Assessment*. In support of the 12-Month Development Plan, the **Development Conversation** and development techniques are also introduced.

Creating the Development Plan

The purpose of a development plan is to document employee goals to fill gaps in the required skills and competencies for a specific position, along with a specific timeline to accomplish the development goals. In Chapter 9, the *SP Employee Competency Assessment* was introduced as a method for analyzing and determining gaps in your employees' competencies and skills. This assessment identified the required development for an employee over the next twelve months.

When you understand the development priorities for the next twelve months, you can create a custom development plan with your employee. The competency and skill gaps need to be addressed with specific development techniques and within a specific time frame to ensure leaders are prepared for success and succession.

It's important the employee be involved in creating their development plan since they are the one who will be doing the heavy lifting. During the **Development Conversation**, if they haven't already been identified as a high potential, listen for statements from your employee that may show you they have potential for more responsibilities. Remember in Chapter 7 we explored how to identify high potentials using the *SP High Potential Identification Worksheet*.

Development Conversation: A time dedicated between the manager and employee to discuss employee development goals, progress being made, and how development is impacting job success. It's also the time to update the employee's development plan.

In Dan's case, his managers would have a 1:1 working session with their employees. During this meeting, they revisited the career conversation in Chapter 7 and confirmed career goals and professional interests of the employee. If your company is practicing EOS®, then your Quarterly 5-5-5™ conversations have a place for areas of development and a plan. I recommend having a separate document specifically for development, The *SP 12-Month Development Plan*, which ties development back to specific organizational and personal goals as well as specific skills and competency gaps. Having a separate and specific development document sends a signal to your employee that their growth is a priority to you and the business, and how their efforts link back to your company's success.

The Development Plan

A good development plan ensures the employee is growing personally and professionally to meet your organizational goals as well as their career goals. Developing employees is a partnership between the employer and the employee and should be mutually beneficial.

While the development plan is co-created between the manager and employee, the employee is the owner of the plan. Creating a development plan is just the beginning. Working the plan and tracking progress as discussed in Chapter 12 is just as important to the development process.

Before meeting with your employee, complete the first three columns of the individual development plan: development goal, relationship of goal to organizational/team goals, and knowledge, skills, and competency gaps to be developed. From the *SP Employee Competency Assessment*, the twelve-month development goals will be transferred to the *SP 12-Month Development Plan* in the developmental goals. This information helps provide you a starting point for the Development Conversation. The other columns will be completed during the conversation.

The *SP 12-Month Development Plan* can be found at the end of this chapter

The Development Conversation

The **Development Conversation** is designed to co-create a development plan with your employee. Make sure you have the employee's *Job Profile* with the documented skills and competencies and their *Performance Conversations documentation* available for reference.

As you have your Development Conversation with your employee, you will be completing the *SP 12-Month Development Plan*, which will be the cornerstone to monitoring development progress in Chapter 12. The conversation will start by reviewing the information already on the form. As you discuss competency and skill gaps, you will come to an agreement on the focus for development over the next twelve months while keeping in mind the company strategy and goals as well as the information from the *SP Employee Competency Assessment*. Reference the performance review and job profile when necessary to support your initial competency assessment.

Once you and your employee are in agreement, determine the start and end dates of the development activity and what specific activities and methods of development will be used to gain the desired knowledge/expertise in the time frame required.

The next section of this chapter contains a comprehensive list of development methods for you to reference as you complete the development plan.

Choosing Development Methods

There is a myriad of methods you can deploy for employee development. Below is a listing of development techniques and programs to help with your employee's development.

Before you choose development methods, however, be clear on what the learning objective is for the employee. When deciding on the timing of development, it's important the development is delivered in a timely manner so your employee can apply his or her learning shortly after they acquire the new knowledge or skills. When choosing the appropriate development method, you should also know how the employee prefers to learn. They generally know what has worked for them in the past, and if they don't I recommend two online quizzes: www.vark-learn.com and www.educationplanner.org to help them determine their preferred learning styles.

Ask yourself the following questions when deciding on development methods:

- What is the learning objective? Hard skill or soft skill?

- When do you need the employee to complete the objective?

- How does the employee best learn? Visual, auditory, verbal (reading/writing), or kinesthetic?

- What is the training budget?

Types of Development Methods

1. **Mentoring (low cost):** Mentoring is designed to share technical, industry, and professional knowledge. It is a unique and personalized process to the development needs of the employee. Mentoring can be informal or formal. Formal programs provide organizations with a method to match more seasoned employees with less experienced employees, whereas informal programs happen organically and a match between mentor and mentee isn't formally created. Mentors can come from inside or outside the organization.

   Mentoring can provide knowledge transfer in a systematic way, structured learning to prepare an employee for new or expanded responsibilities, identification of future high potentials, and a way to learn "soft skills" such as judgement, influence, and executive presence.

2. **Stretch assignments (low cost):** This type of development technique is often used with high potentials. The assignments are unique projects structured to provide challenging experiences to an employee. They are selected to develop specific competencies identified as gaps in the development plan. Additionally, these assignments challenge high potentials, which can assist in retaining your top employees.

3. **Job Enrichment (low cost):** Job enrichment is a process of adding dimensions to a job to make it more

motivating. This technique helps to expand specific skills of an employee by adding extra tasks (job enlargement). While the goal is about motivating an employee vs developing an employee, the secondary goal is skill development.

4. **Cross Training and Knowledge Transfer (low cost):** This development technique is especially important for short-term and long-term results. In Chapter 5, some key positions may have been identified because of specialized knowledge and expertise a specific position required. Without this knowledge, your business operations will be disrupted. Both cross training and knowledge transfer address this potential risk. Cross training is broader in scope than knowledge transfer and prepares the person being cross trained for a specific position. Knowledge transfer focuses on providing specific knowledge to an employee to expand a current role or advance to a more elevated role.

5. **Training and Presenting to Others (low cost):** One of the most overlooked development methods is having an employee train or present to others. For some employees, this may be considered a *stretch assignment*. What best practice or specialized knowledge/skill can an employee present to benefit other employees? What has an employee recently learned that they can share with others? This type of development can provide exponential benefits. Not only does the employee benefit from training others, but the employees receiving the training gain new knowledge.

6. **Book Clubs (low cost):** Organizing a book club helps to increase engagement, align business strategy, and build relationships across departments. They encourage employees to continue to develop professionally and personally. The key is choosing the right books and having a good facilitator for the group. The choice of the book should align with your business goals.

Have your leaders make recommendations first and encourage members to make recommendations once the club is established.

7. **Online resources (low cost):** From TEDx videos to online workshops, online resources provide flexibility and focus for a development plan. Because there are so many options to choose from, it can take time researching them to meet a specific development objective. The upside is most of the resources are free or low-cost. Two of the leaders in the industry are www.Lynda.com and www.Udemy.com .

8. **Coaching (mid cost):** Leadership and executive coaching address the professional aspirations of the employee and focus on learning, staying balanced, and guiding leaders to their full potential through goal setting, self-awareness, and improving certain aspects of performance.

   Coaching is generally provided by external resources, unlike mentoring. External coaches can be unbiased and challenge existing mindsets. However, larger companies often have internal coaches who are trained to deliver coaching to employees. The coaching generally lasts between six–twelve months and is designed to focus on specific gaps an individual needs to close for their existing role or prepare them for their next position.

   Unlike many of the other learning and development techniques, coaching is generally focused on soft skills and helps the coachee to become more self-aware, more self-regulated, and increase their emotional intelligence, empathy, and leadership effectiveness.

9. **Professional Associations (mid cost):** Professional associations are beneficial to employees with functional expertise such as accountants, lawyers, engineers, and human resources. They provide employees

with continuing and advanced education in their professional expertise, and networking opportunities to connect with local and national leaders in their profession. For employees who want to get involved at a higher level as a volunteer, there can be informal leadership development opportunities on committees and boards.

10. **Industry/Trade Associations (mid cost):** Industry associations are great for employees needing to keep up with industry trends and government policies and regulations impacting your industry. They expose members to new ideas they wouldn't be exposed to in your company.

11. **Workshops (mid cost):** This method of development generally addresses a specific skill and may be delivered on-site or off-site. Workshops are usually multiple days in length and created for the general public as opposed to custom-built. Make sure you time these workshops to coincide with a way the employee can put the new skills/knowledge into immediate action following the workshop.

12. **College and University Education (High cost):** One way to invest in your high potentials is through degree and certificate programs offered by colleges and universities. This development option is expensive, especially for smaller companies. Some companies will split the cost with the employee or lock the employee into an employment contract to protect their investment for a certain time period. Should the employee decide to leave before the culmination of the contract, a portion of the tuition is due back to the company.

Coach vs Mentor

While both mentoring and coaching are great methods for development, they are different in approach and the goals that can be accomplished. A coach helps an employee to explore what may be holding them back from their true potential and is often focused on behaviors, not hard skills. Coaches ask questions and challenge self-limiting beliefs. By contrast, a mentor acts as an advocate for the employee's career and will share experiences, skills, and knowledge to benefit in an employee's development.

Learn to Coach

Earlier in the chapter, I stated "it's the job of every leader to develop their employees." The single most important development tool a leader has is coaching. Coaching provides you with a process and techniques to help employees grow and learn in real time. It's important to note employees must be self-aware and open to change if coaching is going to work.

The two most important techniques in coaching are observing and being curious by asking open-ended questions.

- **Observing:** Opportunities to coach your employees will present themselves. Learn to look at situations such as lack of follow through, poor communication, and inability to deal with team conflict as opportunities to provide them with just-in-time guidance. Ask yourself, "Is this a coachable moment?"

- **Ask open-ended questions:** Asking open-ended questions will get your employee to explore options and choose their own solution. For example, asking "How do you think we could improve customer satisfaction?" will get you a more thoughtful answer than "Do you think you could do a better job of responding to customer concerns in a timely manner?" Be forewarned, it will be difficult to let an employee talk it out without jumping in with your own solution! If you lose patience and provide them with an answer, you've robbed them of learning for themselves and they won't commit to the solution in the same way they would if it were their own.

If you are interested in learning more about coaching, I recommend two books: *Coaching for Performance* by John Whitmore and *The Coaching Manager* by James Hunt and Joseph Weintraub.

Coaching not only benefits the employee, but will also enhance your leadership abilities. It will allow you to not only differentiate among employees but also bring a specific skill set to communicating and developing your team on an individual basis.

You now have the appropriate development activity for each goal and documented them on your employee's *SP 12-month Development Plan*. It's time to complete the development plan by determining what resources will be required, when the activity will start and end, and determining how you and the employee will know the new skill or knowledge has been acquired.

Tracking Progress

Once the development plan is completed, you will need to track and monitor progress, which is discussed in Chapter 12. I recommend having a conversation at least quarterly with the employee to discuss their progress and provide any assistance with roadblocks.

Rapid Recall

- A development plan is co-created between the employee and the manager.

- All employees should have development plans, not just high potentials.

- Development plans provide many benefits, including preparing successors for key positions.

- There are a variety of development methods and techniques to fit your training budget and development objectives.

- Coaching is the most important technique for developing employees.

- Progress should be tracked by meeting with the employee at least twice a year.

12-Month Development Plan

Name:		Position:	
Signature:		Date:	
Manager:			
Signature:		Date:	

Developmental goals for the coming year	Relationship of goal to the organization's goals	Knowledge, skills, abilities to be developed	Developmental activity	Resources	Start/End Dates	How will success be verified?
Goal 1						
Goal 2						
Goal 3						

The 12-Month Development Plan is used in conjunction with employee competency assessment, 360° assessment, feedback partner interviews, and performance conversations.

Directions:
Column 1 Development Goals: A specific competency-based goal identified on the Employee Competency Assessment form.

Column 2 Relationship of Goal: How does the development goal relate to the organizational or team goal?

Column 3 Specific Gap Being Filled: Specific skill, knowledge, behavior to be gained through development, information obtained through 360°, feedback partner interviews and performance conversations.

Column 4 Developmental Activities: What type of activities will be needed to fill competency gap in column 3.

Column 5 Resources Required: Specific resources required from manager/organization to support development activity (i.e. budget, management time)

Column 6 Start / End Dates: When will development activity begin and be completed.

Column 7 How Will Success Be Verified: What metrics, systems, processes, or data will be used to verify development has occurred?

INTRODUCTION TO RECRUIT PHASE

In Phase 4: Recruit, you will be attracting and hiring for key positions identified as critical to your succession plan. Ideally, you will have developed your high potential employees to be prepared to step into key positions. However, there will be times when you won't have an employee ready to fill the shoes of a key employee exiting the organization.

During the Recruit Phase, we will discuss how to attract top candidates for key positions, the key mistakes companies make during the hiring process, and how to conduct a behavioral interview, focusing on *how* a candidate has accomplished past success, not *what* they accomplished, and finally how to make the hiring decision.

SP Tools introduced during the RECRUITING phase:

- Hiring Checkup List
- Interview Process Checklist

- Shortlisting Interview Scorecard

Question: How confident are you and your team in your hiring process and the ability to bring on the right employees at the right time to fill the key positions in your Succession Plan?

Warning! Hiring key employees can make or break your succession plan. Hiring success depends on a solid, consistent process and requires hiring managers to be effective at interviewing and making final decisions. Taking shortcuts in the process can have severe consequences in the success of your succession plan.

CHAPTER 11
UNCOVERING EXTERNAL TALENT: HIRING SUCCESS FOR KEY POSITIONS

"People are not your most important asset. The right people are."
~ Jim Collins ~

During his succession planning readiness assessment, Dan's team evaluated their hiring process using the *SP Hiring Checkup List*. They identified areas they needed to shore up before filling some key positions with external hires. The list looked at their organizational processes and systems, how they attracted candidates, and their interviewing and assessment processes to identify hiring process shortcomings. For Dan's company, interviewing and assessment processes had some weaknesses, so they spent time making adjustments that resulted in a stronger, more consistent process used for all candidates. As a result of their efforts, the company increased their hiring success rate.

I recommend you evaluate your hiring process before you want to bring on key employees, and the *SP Hiring Checkup List* is a good place to start. You can find the *SP Hiring Checkup List* at the end of the chapter.

You are now in the Recruit Phase of Succession Planning. Before arriving here, you and your team have done a lot of work to prepare for hiring key employees.

You and your Succession Planning Team have reviewed your Strategic Plan and current Organizational Chart and have redesigned your Organizational Chart to align with future business needs. Your new organizational chart allowed you to assess what positions are key to your success using the *SP Key Role Identification Worksheet*.

In the previous phase, *Analyze,* your team identified competency and skill gaps of employees currently in key positions to incorporate into development plans for employees. Your team also identified your high potentials using the *SP 9-Box Grid* and they were placed on your *SP Organizational Succession Planning Roadmap* based on readiness for future position(s).

Now it's time to attract and hire employees to fill those key roles added to your organization if you have no internal successors identified. Unlike the average hire, filling key positions can make or break your succession plan. Key positions are critical hires.

Take Justin, for example, who decided he needed to hire a successor. Justin founded a telecommunications company back in the '90s. He found himself wanting to spend more time with his family as he entered his sixties. Yet, there was no one in the company who could be his successor, so he went out externally and recruited from within the industry.

While the successor had great experience within the industry, he didn't fit culturally with Justin's company. Justin and his team had not taken the time to identify the core competencies demonstrating company values and specific leadership competencies required for the position. Furthermore, he and his team did not have a set of behavioral interview questions to undercover a candidate's core competencies. Nine months later he had to let his successor go and the timeline for Justin's succession plan was delayed. What was going to be a two-year transition turned out to be close to four years. Don't let this happen to you!

Attracting Great Candidates

There continues to be a shortage of good talent. And you'll probably experience an even greater shortage of talent when it comes to filling key roles in your company because they generally require more experience and/or specific, hard-to-find skills and expertise.

On top of the shortage, you are one of thousands of small businesses trying to attract the same talent. How do you stand out in the crowd and get noticed? There are three techniques all companies, including yours, can employ to attract good candidates:

1. Shape and tell a compelling story about your company and your team. When you are in the community networking or volunteering, be passionate about your company and the values your company stands for and you will attract people who share your values.

2. Have an enjoyable and fun culture, and one that creates a community where people can collaborate and connect. People spend the majority of their waking hours working, so they want the time they spend working to be enjoyable and rewarding.

3. Create a community to attract future employees. This community will be open to those interested in your industry or a specific skill. I've seen companies create meet-up groups where like-minded employees and members of the community share their experiences and knowledge. I've worked with companies who partner with local colleges where employees volunteer, or the company provides scholarships for winners of

contests like hackathons. Companies that develop strong community partnerships get noticed by top talent and are at a competitive advantage.

The position you are trying to fill may require an outside recruiter, either because the expertise you are looking for is unique or the position needs to be backfilled before an internal successor is prepared to take the reins. I would argue if you had a solid, strategic succession plan you have been executing, both of these situations can be avoided.

Your strategic succession plan provides you with time to develop current employees to be prepared for succession or to recruit high potential leaders into your talent pool ready for succession without using a recruiter. How do you find great employees without a recruiter? You use your network. This is the number one hiring mistake small businesses make—not having a network of high potentials. There are several common mistakes business make in hiring, and having a weak network is just one of them.

Key Mistakes in Hiring

A great hiring process will consistently identify the candidates most likely to succeed in the position and culture your company is offering. Use the *SP Hiring Checkup List* Dan and his team used to quickly evaluate the health of your hiring process. Below are the eight most common hiring mistakes I have encountered in smaller companies which, when corrected, will improve your hiring success rate:

1. **Poor network of high potentials:** Some of the very best hires I have seen in smaller companies came from the business owner's personal network. The business owner took on a personal role in networking and spent time nurturing relationships with high-potential candidates. I remember one executive who had known his future VP of Sales for over five years. He watched

his progress and strengthened the relationship over the years, and when his company needed to expand the executive team, he was able to fill this new key position quickly and successfully.

2. **No training:** Few managers are ever trained to interview and select employees. When hiring managers are trained in behavioral interviewing skills, know how to decrease their biases, and assess candidates using a consistent process, your hiring success rate is increased. Most managers I've worked with who have great interviewing skills were previously trained in interviewing and selecting employees. Who in your company hires well? What best practices can other managers learn from those who excel in hiring? The easiest way to get your managers trained up is to identify who can share their knowledge with them.

3. **Lack of formal a process:** Consistent, formal hiring processes are often missing in small to midsize companies. When the interview process is consistent from one department to another, a business will have higher retention rates, consistent assessment, and quicker decisions. Consistency leads to continuous improvement of your hiring process. The *SP Hiring Checkup List* will help you assess your current hiring process to identify gaps you will need to fill.

4. **First Impression Bias:** We have all fallen victim to this bias. We meet someone for the first time and in a matter of seconds, we connect with them or we don't. I personally can remember a number of hires I made in my early years that were a result of first impression bias. You can minimize this bias by challenging your first impressions with a formal plan of asking questions that can change your mind as to whether the first impression was truly positive or negative.

5. **Hiring assessments:** The two common missteps businesses have with hiring assessments are 1) They don't
use one or use one at the wrong time in the hiring
process; and 2) They use one not validated for hiring
purposes.

Hiring assessments are best used before you make a
job offer, not as an afterthought. You may be chuckling
to yourself, but I have had several clients who hired an
employee without including an assessment in the hiring
process and then a month later wanted to have an assessment run on their new employee because of a behavioral
or performance issue. I recommend you incorporate
assessments into your process when you have decided to
invite a candidate back for a second interview.

Hiring assessments can decrease hiring bias and assist
in predicting future job success. A validated assessment
has been scientifically shown to consistently predict job
outcomes.

Two of the most commonly used assessments, Myers-
Briggs and DiSC, while valuable for development and
team building, are not validated for use in the hiring
process. Before using an assessment, check with your
assessment provider to confirm their assessment is validated for pre-employment hiring.

6. **Overselling your company:** Yes, there is a shortage
of talent out there, and it's easy to sugarcoat issues at
your company with a candidate because of this shortage, but this tactic often blows up in your face.

I've heard countless stories from executives who had this
happen to them personally and they didn't last long with
the company. And you can be sure I wasn't the only one
with whom they shared their story. When you sugarcoat

your company culture or the actual job, you end up with a disillusioned employee who becomes disengaged and looking for their next opportunity. Hiring employees is expensive—don't use this tactic to sell a candidate.

7. **Not properly onboarding:** The goal of onboarding is to enable new employees to be as productive as possible in the shortest amount of time, reinforce their decision to join your company, and engage them in your culture and new work relationships. Effective onboarding is one of the most overlooked aspects of talent management. Onboarding should start the day an employee accepts your job offer.

   According to the Human Capital Institute, 58% of companies focus onboarding on process and paperwork. A great onboarding experience will focus on company culture, vision, and values, as well as the employee's needs. A structured program incorporating these components will increase productivity, employee engagement, and retention. A *Harvard Business Review* report showed 33% of employees seek a new job within six months of being hired. A good onboarding program will decrease this risk for your company.

8. **Weighting skills over behavior:** When I was running my consulting company, one of the rules I lived by was you can teach skills, but you can't teach attitude. When hiring, my team spent time uncovering whether a candidate's behaviors aligned with our values and the competencies identified for the specific position. The best way to move to a focus on behaviors is using a **Behavioral Interviewing Process**.

Behavioral Interviewing Process

If there is one thing you can do to improve hiring success, it's focusing on past behaviors of candidates to understand how they achieved and accomplished their goals. When you attract great talent, it doesn't always translate into great talent for your company. The talent may not thrive in your culture. I often use the analogy of the palm tree in Florida. It will thrive in the sun, sand, and humidity, yet if it is transplanted to Alaska it will quickly die. People are the same way. They don't thrive in all cultures and environments.

Understanding how to conduct a behavioral interview will help you to identify candidates who will thrive in your company's culture with the behaviors and competencies you and your company value.

It will take time, training, and discipline to implement and consistently deliver behavioral interviews, but once the process is consistently used your hiring success rate will dramatically increase.

Prepare for the Interview:

There are three important steps to prepare for the actual behavioral interview:

1. Evaluate the skills and competencies of the position

Make a list of the specific skills and behaviors you want the person filling the job to have. Refer back to Chapter 6 when you defined core competencies. Consider what skills and behaviors are necessary for completing tasks in the job, and then consider what obstacles may come up when performing those tasks. If you don't know what challenges are inherent to the job, ask the person leaving the position what they had to overcome to complete their tasks.

2.   Evaluate the needs of your company or team

Your team and company have their own culture and values. Every person has their own best work environment. Determining if your candidate aligns with your values is very important to predicting their success and productivity. Questions you can include in the interview might be "Tell me about a time environment and culture helped you to achieve your goals effectively. Describe the environment. What about another time where the way your office worked hindered your ability to get your job done? Can you give me some examples?" Listen to their answers to see how your culture aligns with their best experiences.

3.   Describe your perfect candidate

Create a description of the ideal candidate for the position so when candidates show those traits, you can compare how close each candidate is to an ideal fit with the job. Consider the team they will be working with and ask for examples of how the candidate previously functioned around people with those personalities and work styles. Determine what competencies and skills will show success in the position. Then develop questions to uncover their past behaviors to see if the candidate has the competencies required to be successful. Knowing what your future employee looks like before the interview means you can recognize them when they tell you about their work, rather than only hoping the person who sounds the most competent really is the right person.

Just because someone's resumé shows they have a great list of experiences doesn't mean they are the ideal person for *your* company. Remember, you don't want a palm tree for Alaska.

Tips for Behavioral Interview Questions

Behavioral questions are designed to uncover past actions and behavior to determine both culture and values fit.

Let's use Dan's competencies to demonstrate how to create behavioral interview questions. In Chapter 6, Dan's team identified the core competencies supporting their values. One of the competencies was Working Together and the three behaviors employees display to support Working Together were the following:

- Works with and supports other team members to drive results.

- Builds two-way relationships with employees and customers.

- Understands and respects other people's priorities.

When delivering a behavioral question, remember to keep the following in mind:

1. Use open-ended questions starting with "What" or "How." Open-ended questions encourage discussion and require people to think and reflect—they aren't recall questions. Recall questions are those that ask someone to remember a person, event, date, place, and so on.

    The very best questions are really a request to share an experience, such as "Tell me about a time…" or "Share an example of…"

2. The question/request should be designed to not "lead the witness."

3. Understand what a good answer sounds like. Listen for the pronoun "I." If you hear "we" being used, you will need to clarify what exactly the job candidate's role was.

As an example, let's use the behavior "Works with and supports other team members to drive results." A good behavioral interview question would be the following:

"Tell me about a time you had to deal with a difficult team member on a project."

If I had adjusted the question to say, "Tell me about a time you had to deal with a difficult team member to **successfully complete** a project," I would have been leading the witness and assuming the project was completed successfully. Give the candidate the opportunity to share with you how the project turned out.

Get candidates to tell their story and ask questions along the way. Re-ask a question to see if you get the same response. A change in response can be a flag the candidate is exaggerating or potentially lying.

The STAR Method

Many candidates have been trained on how to answer an interview question using the STAR Method. The STAR Method goes like this:

Situation: The candidate will describe a situation with relevant details to answer a behavioral question you have asked. Make sure the candidate explains the context of the situation and how it relates to your question.

Task: The candidate will describe their role in the situation. Get clarity on what level of responsibility they had.

Action: Then the candidate will describe what steps they took to resolve the challenge. Understand from them how they made decisions and added value to the situation.

Result: Finally, the candidate will describe the outcome of the situation, providing you with concrete examples and quantifiable results their efforts directly affected and what they learned through the process.

As the interviewer, you should be prepared to walk a candidate through the STAR method if they are not familiar with it.

Let's go back to the question: "Tell me about a time you had to deal with a difficult team member on a project." This question was designed to determine a candidate's experience in "Working with and supporting other team members to drive results."

As the interviewer, listen for an answer that covers the Situation, Task, Action, and Result, and that demonstrates the candidate has been able to work with team members to drive results. You should listen for behaviors and actions that demonstrate the other two behaviors associated with your company value of Working Together:

o Builds two-way relationships with employees and customers.

o Understands and respects other people's priorities.

This question can also illuminate how the candidate deals with conflict since they had to work with a difficult employee. Well-crafted behavioral interview questions can uncover more than one competency important to the position.

While Behavioral Interviewing is the foundation to a good interviewing process, there are other elements to interviewing that when consistently used will ensure good results. I recommend using the *SP Interview Process Checklist* before inviting a candidate in for an interview. It will help you and your team be prepared to deliver consistent interviews. The checklist can be found at the end of the chapter.

Making the Hiring Decision

Once you have a consistent hiring process and managers know how to deliver a behavioral interview, then it's time to make your hiring decision. The *SP Shortlisting Interview Scorecard* helps you organize the results of your interviews to make a solid hiring decision. The Scorecard can be found at the end of the chapter.

Rapid Recall

- Use the *SP Hiring Checkup List* to identify any gaps in your hiring process.

- To attract great candidates, create a compelling company story, have a culture people want to be a part of, and create a community that attracts future employees.

- Avoid the top eight hiring mistakes many small businesses make.

- Improve hiring decisions by using a behavioral interviewing process.

- Prepare for the interview by evaluating the skills and competencies of the position and the needs of the company/team, and then describe your perfect candidate.

- Create behavioral interview questions to uncover past behaviors and actions to determine culture, values, and competency fit.

- Use the STAR Method (Situation, Task, Action, Result) to listen for the behaviors you are looking for in a candidate.

- Use the *SP Interview Process Checklist* to deliver a consistent interview experience

- Use the *SP Shortlisting Interview Score Card* to assist in your decision-making process

HIRING CHECK UP LIST

Today's job market is candidate-driven and hiring quality candidates is hard with talent at a premium. So, your hiring process should run like an efficient "well-oiled machine." The hiring process is composed of your company's organizational process supporting hiring and the hiring phases: Attracting Candidates, Interviewing Candidates, Assessing Candidates, and Closing the Deal.

If you and your team are responsible for hiring great talent and aren't getting the hiring results you need, use this checklist as a starting point to determine gaps in your process. Then make a plan to fill the gaps.

ORGANIZATIONAL HIRING PROCESS   Yes   No
- Are you able to fill positions in a timely manner?   ☐   ☐
- Have you lost candidates because your hiring process was too slow? ☐   ☐
- Is the job description current, clear and concise, with specific success
  metrics and performance standards?   ☐   ☐
- Do you have a consistent recruiting process across the organization? ☐   ☐
- Is the recruiting process documented?   ☐   ☐
- Do all managers understand the steps in your hiring process?   ☐   ☐
- Do you have strategic relationships externally for attracting talent? ☐   ☐
- Do you have and track hiring metrics?   ☐   ☐

HIRING PHASES:

ATTRACTING   Yes   No
- Are your job postings enticing to applicants?   ☐   ☐
- Are you actively promoting your company in the community?   ☐   ☐
- Is your applicant pipeline filled with quality applicants?   ☐   ☐
- Is your online reputation attracting applicants?   ☐   ☐
- Are all of your employees part of the recruiting process?   ☐   ☐

INTERVIEWING

	Yes	No
• Do you have a defined phone screening process?	☐	☐
• Are candidates clear on the steps in your interview process?	☐	☐
• Do you have an interviewing plan?	☐	☐
• Are all hiring managers trained in hiring and behavioral interviewing of candidates?	☐	☐
• Are teams used to interview candidates?	☐	☐
• Do you have a company story used to help "sell" candidates?	☐	☐
• Do you have a personal story of what makes working for your company rewarding?	☐	☐
• Are you identifying the candidates' pain points for use to close them later?	☐	☐
• Is your interviewing process always closing the candidate?	☐	☐

ASSESSING

	Yes	No
• Do you use assessment tools validated for hiring to decrease bias in your hiring process?	☐	☐
• Is more than one person involved in assessing candidates?	☐	☐
• Are your candidates' values aligned with the organization?	☐	☐
• Do you have a structured method of comparing candidates?	☐	☐
• Do you call all references?	☐	☐
• Do you have other options to verify skills other than references?	☐	☐

CLOSING THE DEAL

	Yes	No
• Is the offer being made in a timely manner?	☐	☐
• Is your offer resolving their pain points identified in the interviewing process?	☐	☐
• Are your salaries and benefits competitive in the market?	☐	☐
• Do you make your potential employee feel special and wanted?	☐	☐
• Are you describing what their career path will be?	☐	☐
• Does your onboarding process start before the employee's first day?	☐	☐

INTERVIEW PROCESS CHECKLIST

Week before the Interview:
- ☐ Create a file of candidate's documents for review: application forms, resume, cover letter, etc.
- ☐ Review candidate's application. Determine questions you need to ask about career history: gaps in employment, changes of career, etc.
- ☐ Review behavioral interview questions.
- ☐ Double-check your questions to see if any could be misconstrued as offensive and/or discriminatory.
- ☐ Prepare to answer likely questions the candidate may have for you about the job, the department, and the company.
- ☐ Be aware of the next steps in the interview/selection process so you can communicate them to the candidate at the end of the interview.
- ☐ Schedule room or video for interview.
- ☐ Coordinate schedules with other interviewers.

Day before the Interview:
- ☐ Confirm timing of interviews for the following day with other participants.
- ☐ Check interview room and ensure it is clean and free from distracting and/or confidential materials.

Day of Interview:
- ☐ Arrange furniture in interview room so candidates will be relaxed and comfortable.
- ☐ Notify appropriate colleagues you will be conducting interviews and can't be disturbed.
- ☐ Bring *Interview Scorecard* and *list of Behavioral Questions* and candidate file.
- ☐ Bring *Interview Agenda.*

After the Interview:
- ☐ Review your notes and scorecard to select a final candidate OR meet with hiring team to review and select a final candidate.
- ☐ Proceed with checking references, background checks, MVR, and/or drug screen if appropriate.
- ☐ Through the entire interview/selection process, hiring managers should stay in touch with the candidates interviewed via phone and email.
- ☐ Decide what offer to make to the final candidate.
- ☐ Make formal offer of employment to the selected candidate. Once the offer is accepted, provide the candidate with offer letter and move to onboarding process.
- ☐ Send out rejection letters to candidates interviewed to let them know a decision has been made.
- ☐ Place the remaining candidates in the applicant pool not selected for interview at the appropriate "not hired" reason. The only candidates(s) remaining in the process will be those hired.

SHORTLISTING INTERVIEW SCORECARD

Directions for using the Shortlisting Interview Scorecard

Making a hiring decision is one of the hardest and costliest decisions a manager can make. This scorecard is designed to help you and your team compare multiple candidates for a specific position before making your hiring decision.

The hiring manager or Human Resources will fill in the top row of the table with the appropriate educational level, top experiences, skills, and culture fit which will correlate to company values. You can determine culture fit by using behavioral interview questions. The template is provided as a starting point and additional columns can be added to the scorecard. If you add columns you will need to adjust the TOTAL POINTS column.

If there is more than one person interviewing, each person interviewing will fill out the form for every candidate and as a group you can compare the results and discuss differences to come to a final hiring decision.

Completing the scorecard will provide you with the knowledge for making a good hiring decision amongst several candidates.

Job Title:

Name of Candidate	Education Level 1 = min 2 = desired	Experience 1 = min 2 = mid-point 3 = exceeds	Experience 1 = min 2 = mid-point 3 = exceeds	Skills 0 = poor 1 = average 2 = strong	Skills 0 = poor 1 = average 2 = strong	Culture Fit 0 = poor 1 = average 2 = strong	TOTAL POINTS (3–12)

INTRODUCTION TO RECOGNIZE PHASE

The final phase in succession planning has two steps: 1) Monitoring and Assessing the development progress of employees; and 2) Recognizing and Rewarding the success of meeting goals.

During the first step of monitoring and assessing you will be monitoring the development progress of your high potentials through quarterly development conversations. In your semi-annual talent conversations you'll make promotion and job rotation decisions while also updating your *SP Organizational Succession Planning Roadmap*. The Succession Planning Team will also measure the effectiveness of your Succession Planning process for continuous improvement.

The final step is celebrating all the success achieved by both employees and your team through recognition and rewards.

Question: Do you and your team know if a high potential employee is ready to move into a new position? How effective is your succession planning process? And how are you recognizing individual and team success?

Warning! This last phase in succession planning requires a commitment of time to have quarterly conversations. Plan them out in advance and make the time sacred for you and the employee. Reschedule only for dire emergencies. Celebrate success when its achieved.

CHAPTER 12

IS THERE PROGRESS? MONITORING AND ASSESSMENT OF EMPLOYEES AND THE TEAM

"For changes to be of any true value, they've
got to be lasting and consistent."

~ Tony Robbins ~

Your team has reached the point in Succession Planning where you need to monitor the progress of your high potentials and key employees as they execute their development plans. Without a solid process of monitoring and assessing progress, promotion and job rotation decisions will be at risk. It is also the time to measure your succession planning process and document changes needed to improve.

When Dan's team arrived at this final step, they had made investments in a talent management system to provide an integrated platform to assist in tracking performance and development. Because of the new talent management system, they were able to eliminate some of the forms introduced throughout this book.

MEASURING TALENT DEVELOPMENT

If you don't have an integrated system, you will need these forms, introduced earlier, to properly assess the development of your employees:

- *SP Organizational Succession Planning Roadmap*: Use this form to move candidates up in readiness based on development success.

- *SP 12-Month Development Plans*: Verify success by success metrics in the plan and the development timeline.

- *SP 9-Box Grid*: Based on development and performance, should they be reassigned to a different box on the grid? If so, share your insights during the Talent Conversation and make the necessary adjustments.

You and your team have invested both time and money in developing your employees, especially those in key positions being prepared to step into another role. It's important to have a process to monitor and assess the development of your employees.

Remember, employees want to be developed, and high potential employees won't stick around if they don't believe you are committed to their professional growth. Consistently tracking the development progress of your employees will demonstrate to them you are committed to their success. The benefit will be driving higher retention rates with your "A" players.

Bi-Annual Talent Pool Conversations

Unlike the Quarterly Conversation between you and your employee, the Talent Pool Conversation in Chapter 8 brings together your leadership team to discuss performance and development of key employees and high potentials. These conversations will be held twice a year and serve as a method of assessing an employee's development progress. Dan's team scheduled these conversations each year as part of their planning process to ensure they happened.

Refer back to Chapter 8 for a sample agenda of the Talent Pool Conversation. The goal of these ongoing conversations is to review the *SP 9-Box Grid* and make adjustments based on performance, potential, and development. The changes to the *SP 9-Box Grid* will become part of your quarterly development conversations with your employee.

Quarterly Conversations

Dan's team had implemented quarterly conversations with employees years before they implemented succession planning in their organization. At first, quarterly conversations were strictly focused on past and future performance.

Once they had identified and defined their core competencies, they incorporated competencies into the performance conversation. Including core competencies gave the performance management process a more consistent method of evaluating performance. Also, since the competencies aligned with company values, it was a way to assess an employee's current fit in the organization.

During quarterly conversations, be sure to set aside time to discuss your employee's development plan. Your employee can report back to you on what they accomplished in their development plan and most importantly what they are doing differently since receiving the development. Without change, development hasn't occurred.

If you're a disciple of EOS®, then you're familiar with the 5-5-5™ or Quarterly Conversation. While the process of asking "What's working and what's not working" is good a start, it misses the Development and Career Conversations necessary to keep employees engaged. Career Conversations don't need to happen on a quarterly basis, but a review of an employee's development plan will be part of your quarterly conversation.

The *SP 9-Box Grid* is a great visual tool to use during the Quarterly Conversation. You can share with the employee where they're currently at based on their development and performance as it relates to the nine boxes.

Effectiveness of Development Plans

How do you know if development is working for an employee? How can you measure improvement and progress?

The development plan will have identified success factors for the employee's development objectives. Those success factors need to be measured through tests, stretch assignments, projects, *360° assessments*, and feedback from *Feedback Partners*.

When it comes to core competencies for a position, you can measure change through a 360° assessment. The 360° assessment was introduced back in Chapter 9 to assist in analyzing competency gaps to be addressed in employee development plans. You can remeasure those competencies targeted for development by running another abridged 360° assessment.

If you didn't use a 360° assessment, Feedback Partners are a valuable resource in understanding development effectiveness. To make feedback meaningful, it is important they understand what changes in the behaviors, skills, and results an employee is working on and how to provide the feedback to you.

Making Talent Decisions

The ultimate purpose of monitoring and assessing employees' development is to gather the necessary information to make decisions on talent redeployment to meet the timeline in your *SP Organizational Succession Planning Roadmap*.

These decisions are important to both the employee and the organization. Moving employees into more challenging roles should be done at a time when they are prepared to be stretched, not broken. Each employee has a different stretch point, and your job is to make sure they are stretched to their full potential.

HOW SUCCESSFUL IS THE PROCESS?

Planning is a complex process, so it's just as important to measure your team's performance as well as your employees' development.

As with any process, it's important to measure effectiveness. For Succession Planning the metrics used to measure your Succession Planning Process are the following:

- Complete Implementation of Each Phase of the Process.

- Development Plans Created and Updated.

- Development Progress by Employees.

- Timely meetings: Semi-annual talent discussions, Quarterly Development Conversations, Career Conversations, Promotions, and Job Expansion.

Use the *SP Succession Planning Checklist* to measure your implementation of each phase of the process.

Once the metrics have been complied, the Succession Planning team can assess where they need to improve in the process and make the necessary adjustments before the next planning cycle begins.

Rapid Recall

- Making good decisions on promotions and job rotations requires solid monitoring and assessing of employee progress and development.

- Use the Organizational Succession Planning Roadmap, 12-Month Development Plan, and 9-Box Grid to assess employee progress.

- Attention to the development progress demonstrates to high potentials you are committed to their success.

- Both talent pool and quarterly conversations assist in monitoring employee development.

- Make Talent Pool Conversations part of your business planning process.

- Measure the effectiveness of development plans with abridged 360° assessments and Feedback Partners.

- Use development and meeting metrics to measure the success of your succession planning process and make necessary changes for continuous improvement.

- Use the Succession Planning Checklist, at the end of this chapter, to keep track of your progress.

CHAPTER 13
RECOGNIZING SUCCESS: CELEBRATE!

"People work for money but go the extra mile
for recognition, praise and rewards."

~ Dale Carnegie ~!

Congratulations! You have arrived at the final step of Strategic Succession Planning. This is the time to recognize and celebrate success for your team and those employees who have been elevated or given more responsibilities.

Don't be one of the 65% of managers, according to Gallup, who don't provide any form of recognition to their employees. You and your team have put in a significant amount of time and resources to get to this final step in the process. Skipping this step can wipe out your investment. Increasing retention is a benefit of the succession planning process, and when you practice recognizing success, it's estimated 50% of your employees will stay longer at your company.

There is no "one size fits all" secret method for employee recognition programs. The secret of a great employee recognition program is to fit it to your employees' wants and needs. There are those employees who desire public recognition while others prefer more private recognition. There are employees who value intrinsic over extrinsic rewards. Before rewarding and recognizing employees, you need to understand your employees' unique desires.

The type of employee recognition program your company will offer depends on a variety of factors, including the following:

- Budget
- Number of employees
- Company values
- Core competencies
- Company culture

Many companies don't consider their values and culture when recognizing employees for their success. For those who do stay true to company values and culture, their rewards and recognition programs will reinforce their values and culture.

Succession Planning Team Success

Dan and his team recognized the value of celebrating success, especially when it came to employees' accomplishments and success. However, they didn't understand the value of recognizing their own success as well.

How do you know when to recognize and celebrate success as a team? During your Talent Conversation refer to the completed *SP Organizational Succession Planning Roadmap* from the previous Talent Conversation to determine which high potentials are closer to being prepared to succeed into a key position. High potential development within the pre-determined timeline is how you measure your succession planning team's success.

It goes without saying that team recognition should be as a group because success was a result of the entire team's work. Whether your team is located in a single office or in several offices, these celebrations can work in-person or virtually.

Recognition should be communicated to the entire company with announcements of promotions and job rotations.

Individual Success

Whether it's a high potential or another employee in your talent pool, those who have completed their development plan should be recognized for their accomplishments. One of the top reasons why employees leave their jobs is that they don't feel appreciated, according to Gallup.

And according to an OfficeVibe study, 82% of employees think it's better to give someone praise than a gift. There are many methods you can use to recognize success depending on the employee's wants and needs.

Dan's team had what they believed was a good rewards and recognition program. However, they had experienced turnover of a few high-potential employees they had invested in, so they brainstormed the problem and decided they needed to customize their rewards and recognitions to individual employees and not make it a one-size-fits-all approach.

They then asked the following five questions for each employee:

1. How does the employee like to be recognized, in public or privately?

2. What intangible rewards will be the most meaningful to the employee?

3. What tangible rewards match the accomplishment of the employee?

> 4. What tangible rewards will be impactful to the employee?
>
> 5. Will the rewards given be viewed as fair and equitable by the employee?

How to Recognize Success

Ideas for employees who need public recognition:

- **Surprise appreciation celebration**
  Organize a surprise party for your top performers! Include some cake, confetti, and their favorite tunes.

- **Social Media Shoutouts**
  Post a photo along with their achievements (promotion, certification, significant accomplishment) of your employees on social media.

- **Newsletter**
  Feature your employees' success stories in your company's newsletter.

- **Congratulatory email**
  Send a company-wide congratulatory email from the CEO to recognize employees for a job well done.

- **Press Release**
  Share a story of your employees' success with your local press. When the story is published in the newspaper, get the article framed and give it as a gift to your employees.

Ideas for employees who need private recognition:

- **Handwritten Thank You**
  Send your employees a handwritten note, or just leave a sticky note saying "Thank you" on their desk.

- **Face to Face Thank You**
Ask an employee to your office just to say thanks for a job well done.

- **Send a video**
Create an appreciation video for your employee that includes a thank you message from your CEO.

- **Delivery of Gift**
Have a gift delivered to your employee's house that is meaningful to them.

Ideas for employee intangible rewards:

- **New job position**
Reward your employee with a new, advanced job title.

- **Ambassador opportunity**
Offer your employees the chance to represent your company at an event they typically would not attend.

- **Ask for their help or opinion**
Ask employees for their input on important business issues and show them you value their opinions.

- **Special project**
Give your employees an opportunity to work on special projects beyond their regular responsibilities to give them more visibility.

- **Executive Meeting Invitation**
Invite high potentials to join your executive team meeting.

Ideas for employee tangible awards:

- **Increase in pay**
Show your appreciation by giving your employees a raise.

- **Bonus check**
  When an employee successfully completes a project impacting the company, deliver a bonus check.

- **Vacation**
  Book a luxury vacation for your employees in some exotic destination.

- **Exclusive event tickets**
  Reward your employees with courtside seats of a game, VIP access to a concert that is sold out, or movie tickets to a premiere.

- **Offer educational opportunities**
  Surprise your employees with tickets for a conference, external certification, seminar, training, or other educational opportunities.

Recognition and Rewards Program Success

Recognition programs should be well-funded, aligned with organizational goals, appropriate for employees' achievements, and timely. The methods of presenting awards must be managed well, with managers themselves playing key roles. The process for choosing and recognizing employees should be straightforward, and the program should be reviewed and evaluated regularly.

Evaluating Your Program

Programs must be monitored continually for relevance. Employers should consider asking the following seven questions when evaluating their programs:

1. Are the program's rewards adequate, fair, competitive, and appropriate?

2. Are the program's goals and objectives being met?

3. Is the program improving processes in the organization, and does it support improved performance?

4. Are employees learning about success with appropriate communications?

5. Are there celebrations?

6. Do employees find the program motivating and meaningful?

7. What changes should be made?

The evaluation process should be done annually or semi-annually or semi-annually, so adjustments can be made to improve the system and retain employees' interest.

Individualizing your rewards and recognition program is the key to a successful program. When implemented and executed well, these programs can help retain the high potentials you have invested in developing.

Rapid Recall

- Customized employee recognition programs can increase your retention of high potential employees.

- Celebrate both your succession planning team's success as well as individual employees.

- Determine who needs public versus private recognition.

- Blend both tangible and intangible rewards in your rewards program.

- Evaluate your program by asking seven key questions.

- Make necessary adjustments based on your evaluation.

CONCLUSION: DAN OR RICK? THE CHOICE IS YOURS

I opened this book with a tale of two companies. Dan's company put the time and effort into succession planning and reaped its many rewards. Rick's company did not and was shuttered within eighteen months of his untimely death. Strategic succession planning is the deciding factor in whether your business will not only survive but thrive even when one or more key positions suddenly become vacant.

You can think of a succession plan like an insurance policy. Whether it's health insurance, car insurance, or life insurance, these policies are meant to help make sure you or loved ones have assistance in weathering a crisis. A solid succession plan can do that for your business.

The difference, of course, is in the time and effort it takes to do succession planning right. It's not nearly as easy as paying a monthly premium on an insurance policy. If, however, you want your business to continue on without you; if you want to give your business the greatest chance of continuing to be a place of meaningful work for its employees, then you owe it to yourself and to them to begin the succession planning process sooner rather than later.

This book has presented a succession planning model with six phases: Prepare, Identify, Analyze, Develop, Recruit, and Recognition. Each phase was broken down into steps and the specific tools you need to work through each phase of the succession planning process. If you've made it to this final part of the book, then you now know exactly what's involved in doing succession planning right.

So, what'll it be—Dan or Rick? The choice is yours, and now is the time to decide.

Get expert guidance on succession planning and better hiring at www.executive-velocity.com

APPENDIX: GLOBAL LIST OF COMPETENCIES

Competency	Competency Description
Accountability	Taking responsibility for performance
Adaptability	Exhibiting flexibility toward changes
Analytical Thinking	Analyzing and synthesizing information to understand issues, identify options, and support sound decision making
Attention to Detail	Working in a conscientious, consistent and thorough manner
Building Teams	Creating productive and effective work groups
Change Leadership	Managing organizational change for accelerated impact and reduced friction
Client Focus	Providing service excellence to internal and/or external clients
Coaching	Working with staff to identify strengths and maximize talents

Collaboration	Working with others to accomplish common goals
Collaborative Leadership	Seeking and embracing cooperation among peers in decision making
Communication	Listening to others and communicating effectively
Conflict Management	Working to bring disagreements to resolution
Conscientiousness	Acting in a principled manner
Consulting Skills	Providing high-quality consulting services to clients
Continuous Improvement	Constantly seeking ways to increase effectiveness or reduce costs
Continuous Learning	Keeping up-to-date on relevant current knowledge and skills to perform more effectively
Creativity and Innovation	Creating new approaches and solutions to challenges
Customer Service	Providing customers with a high-quality experience
Delegation	Working through others to maximize productivity
Drive	Demonstrating passion for performance and a desire for continuous improvement
Entrepreneurship	Developing innovative ideas that provide increased value
Fiscal Management	Managing financial resources responsibly
Follow-up	Ensuring work is completed accurately and within established timeframes
Influencing Others	Influencing and gaining the support of others
Initiative	Handling situations and issues proactively
Integrity	Acting in a consistent, principled manner
Interpersonal Skills	Relating to others

Interviewing Skills	Selecting high-quality candidates
Judgment	Makes decisions wisely, after evaluating all available options
Meeting Leadership	Organizing and leading effective team meetings
Meeting Participation	Participating actively and appropriately in meetings
Motivating Others	Creating and sustaining a culture that encourages others to do their best
Negotiation	Creating agreements that maximize benefit to the organization

Competency	Competency Description
Performance Management	Ensuring regular management and communication of employee performance
Political Savvy	Understanding of political landscape within the organization
Presentation Skills	Presenting information effectively to an audience
Problem Solving	Identifying problems and appropriate solutions
Professionalism	Behaving in a manner that upholds the principles of the organization
Project Management	Demonstrating the knowledge and ability to develop a project plan and oversee implementation
Quality	Produces deliverables that meet or exceed expectations
Recruiting	Finding and attracting qualified job candidates
Relationship Building	Establishing professional contacts to build, enhance and connect networks for work purposes
Reliability	Dependability in completing job tasks
Resource Planning	Developing, implementing, evaluating and adjusting plans to reach goals
Results-focus	Planning, organizing and implementing projects to meet established goals
Risk Taking	Taking measured and calculated risks
Self-confidence	Demonstrating realistic confidence in one's abilities
Self-management	Works without the need for constant supervision
Service	Dedication to meeting needs of others in the organization
Strategic Thinking	Understanding and processing complex information with regard to long-term planning
Stress Tolerance	Handling of adverse or stressful situations
Team Leadership	Assuming a leadership role in helping others achieve results

Teamwork	Working collaboratively with others to achieve organizational goals
Technical Expertise	Use of specialized skills and knowledge in the completion of job tasks
Time Management	Effectively managing time in order to accomplish work
Trustworthiness	Acting in a dependable, honest and reliable manner
Vision	Focusing on and crafting the organization's future
Writing Skills	Communicating ideas and information effectively in writing

Made in the USA
Columbia, SC
26 September 2021